What people are saying about

In Praise of Friendship

Michał Herer has written an important book, the subject of which is the late-modern crisis of friendship. Friendship, conceived here as a complex dialectical play between intimacy and distance, possesses a certain je ne sais quoi, an indefinable quality, which binds singulars in a singular manner – and because of that falls out of the charts of the modern society which now is achieving its peak of the Weberian disenchantment and rationalisation.

This little book is remarkably well written; by avoiding jargon and going straight into the essential matter of things, it reads smoothly as a convincing argument.

Professor Agata Bielik-Robson, Professor of Jewish Studies, Theology and Religious Studies, University of Nottingham, UK

This essay shows the erudition of the author, freely moving from the ancient to modern approaches to the concept of friendship, but it develops mostly his idea of renewing this concept in the context of contemporary moral, social and political problems.

The text is philosophical but accessible also to a larger public. Its significance is surely universal.

Małgorzata Kowalska, Professor of Philosophy, University of Białystok

T0163418

In Praise
of Friendship

In Praise
of Friendship

Michał Herer

Translated by Arthur Barys

Winchester, UK
Washington, USA

JOHN HUNT PUBLISHING

First published by Zero Books, 2021
Zero Books is an imprint of John Hunt Publishing Ltd., No. 3 East St., Alresford,
Hampshire SO24 9EE, UK
office@jhpbooks.com
www.johnhuntpublishing.com
www.zero-books.net

For distributor details and how to order please visit the 'Ordering' section on our website.

Text copyright: Michał Herer 2019

ISBN: 978 1 78904 389 1
978 1 78904 390 7 (ebook)
Library of Congress Control Number: 2020933331

A CIP catalogue record for this book is available from the British Library.

Design: Stuart Davies

UK: Printed and bound by CPI Group (UK) Ltd, Croydon, CR0 4YY
Printed in North America by CPI GPS partners

We operate a distinctive and ethical publishing philosophy in
all areas of our business, from our global network of authors to
production and worldwide distribution.

Contents

For Ewa

Chapter 1

How to Live Together

For there is nothing so characteristic of friends as living together.
Aristotle, Nicomachean Ethics

The crisis of community is one to which we have grown accustomed. And no wonder: it is, after all, one of the defining elements of modernity. The modern world provides exceedingly little space for communities based on kinship or shared religion and tradition; it is a world that yields to other forms of collective existence. These new groups are rather associations of individuals who adhere to certain formal (above all, legal) principles stemming from the social contract. A discussion of this profound transformation—the shift from the community to the association as the model of collective living definitive of modernity—would fill the shelves of a large library. The books that discuss, less directly, the psychological, existential, aesthetic, and other aspects of this process, its short and long-term repercussions, as well as the indisputable advantages and benefits it offers the modern individual, freed from the restrictive shackles of bygone forms of community life, would require even more space. Even the phenomena that have propelled us into the phase of late modernity or postmodernism, as some have argued, seem to have had little substantial effect in this regard. No neo-tribal tendencies, no re-awakenings of local cultures, and no religious revivals have managed to change the fact that we are living in an era marked by the crisis of traditional communities. Perhaps it is because this notion of the decline of the community has become so commonplace, so familiar, that we have failed to perceive the nature of another, more recent, crisis, that has already left its mark on our lives. This other crisis is even more fundamental, in that it is not so much a consequence of our abandonment of traditional forms, but a result of our struggles with modern forms of socialization. The crucial question, therefore, is no longer: What happened to the communities of the past? The problem we face is even more elementary, and at once broader, and can be summarized as follows: *How do we live together?*

Yet it is surprising how little attention this problem has drawn from philosophers, especially considering the alarm and concern raised in think pieces, popular social analyses, and even self-help books, all of which repeat the same refrain: We don't know how to live together, how to be couples, how to be married (what with the deregulation of the system of gender roles), or how to form a society (in the face of waning social trust) or a political community (now that politics and PR have become indiscernible). The title of this chapter is borrowed from Roland Barthes, who in 1977 gave a series of lectures at the Collège de France titled *Comment vivre ensemble*, or *How to Live Together*. Naturally, many analyses have been written of all types of social processes and phenomena, that is, those that pertain to humans being together. The mechanisms underlying collective entities in their myriad forms have been studied and described in academic terms, but there is something else at stake in the problem Barthes articulated 4 decades ago. It is a problem that has not been examined as often as it deserves to be, at least not in the realm of philosophy. "How to live...," like Lenin's famous question "What is to be done?" (posed earlier by Chernyshevsky), is a matter that is faced by a subject and at once concerns a certain subject. And yet, unlike the subjects of revolutionary literature, the subject implied in Barthes' question isn't one who knows the answer and proceeds to impart his strategic or tactical knowledge on the reader, with whom he shares a specific, common goal. On the contrary: Éric Marty, the French publisher of Barthes' lecture notes,[1] points out that the dominant mood among the audience was one of disappointment. "That disappointment," Marty writes, "is not only something Barthes anticipated but also, in a certain sense, something he sought."[2] Although the title Barthes proposed does not end with the appropriate punctuation mark, it is an interrogative statement, a question whose answer he did not know; the lecture series was itself a peculiar meditation on the absence, the impossibility of a response. Instead of a utopia, a project, or at least an analysis of some specific form of being together, the renowned semiotician merely offers, in his words, a "phantasm," one that he oddly names *idiorhythmy*. We will return later to this concept and to the notion of a community that is founded, paradoxically enough, on distance, thus allowing its members to retain their "individual rhythms."[3] The very fact that Barthes is forced to approach the matter of living together by using paradoxes and phantasms is itself significant.

Why is it that, despite our increasingly profound and detailed understanding of the mechanisms underlying collective action, group dynamics, and other similar phenomena, it has become increasingly difficult for us, as living, acting subjects, to answer this question, both in theoretical and practical terms? And is this not one source of the fundamental problem that has long scuttled every political philosophy that has set out to fix the world by more or less reasonable means, but without figuring out how to construct a political subject that could pose an actual threat to the status quo? A subject that could challenge, if only in the smallest degree, the power of *Monsieur le Capital*? No collective political subject can emerge in a place where people have no idea how to live together, and where the very word "collective" has ominous overtones. How did we end up in this situation? To understand our predicament, we must return for a moment to the matter of modernity—or, more specifically, to the solutions modernity has always proposed for the alienation for which it was itself partially culpable. Unanchored from their traditional communities and cast into the whirl of market competition—or at least into the whirl of contractually regulated actions whose fundamental objective was the pursuit of personal gain, even in the broadest sense of the term—individuals had to receive not so much an ersatz version of their erstwhile community lives, as the chance to belong to communities that were just as strong and substantial as the ones that they had abandoned. These alternative substantial communities (that is, ones not based exclusively on voidable contracts) were ready and waiting. These were (and, to some extent, still are): the *family* and the *nation*. Both the family and monarchies existed in the pre-modern world, of course, but the nuclear bourgeois family[4] and the nation state are inventions of modernity, modern forms of community in which the individual becomes more than just a vehicle for labor power and creates their own substantial ties to others, living *with* them, not just *among* them. The fact that the alienation of the individual in the economic realm or the individual's status as an "entrepreneur of the self"[5] and their affiliation with a particular family community are just two sides of the same coin is best illustrated by the famous quotation from Margaret Thatcher: "There's no such thing as society. There are individual men and women and there are families." There are individual men and individual women in the market, but they still live together, in families. This concern for the existence of the family is used to justify and excuse the ruthless rivalry between individuals within the bounds of the market. And it is on the "bosom" of the family that men and women take shelter (though not invariably, and not to the same degree) from the world, which they perceive to be indifferent at best, and hostile at worst. The motto of the modern family would read: "United against the world." At the same time, this gesture constitutes a functional element of the whole against which it is aimed. All other ways of living together—or society, to use Thatcher's term—are nothing more than hindrances, and risk being used as grounds for further demands. As long as there exist only individuals and (their) families, and all other non-familial manifestations of common life and action are effectively suppressed or at least marginalized, everything is all right. In this sense, those who complain that modern-day capitalism is destroying the family are at least guilty of oversimplification. To be sure, the perpetual debt, precarious employment, and demands for constant availability that plague today's workers are hardly conducive to a happy family life. It is even more tragic, therefore, that in late modernity a person may struggle against an alien, hostile world, working hard to put food on their family's table, and be left with neither the time nor the energy to live with their husband or wife and—possibly— children. The same is true of the nation. The death of the nation state—not the nation itself—was frequently proclaimed early in the era of globalization (or perhaps at the onset of its latest, current phase). It became something of a ritual to point out that the growing might of the multinational corporation would diminish the nation state's previous significance, and that the latter was practically incapable of regulating the flow of financial capital. All of this is true: the sovereignty of the nation, especially in the economic sense, is becoming a myth before our very eyes, and yet—or perhaps for this very reason—nations and their states are in no hurry to shuffle off the stage of history. In fact, they appear to grow more attached to their "essence," "values," and "traditions" even as their actual relevance shrinks. It is becoming increasingly apparent that all of Europe is being swept by a revival of nationalist sentiments or the rebirth of a cultural chauvinism that rises not to protect national values, but to defend Western "Judeo-Christian" culture from the threats of Islam, immigrants, etc.[6] Multinational corporations have yet to show any concern over this resurgent strain of chauvinism, which at any rate appears to pose little threat to the unrestricted flow of capital. The latter knows no borders, unlike people, who threaten the integrity of "our" culture or some nation or other. The nation state, whose withering away was proclaimed by the prophets of the global village, is similarly alive and well, unlike the European Union, which faces the specter of more "exits." Rather, it may turn out that Deleuze and Guattari were correct when they posited, already in the 1970s, that the nation state, with its attendant bureaucracy, police, and apparatus of violence, was a necessary condition for the implementation of the principles of the capitalist market on a given territory.[7] What comes across as archaic, a relic of a bygone era, is revealed to be perfectly suited to function in our new reality.

The family community and the community of the nation: these are the two perpetually privileged places in which modern man can feel like something more than a cog in a machine, a parameter in an equation that has not been revealed to him, a sapient animal fighting to survive in an economic jungle. This is where he can cultivate values. These places share at least one characteristic with traditional, pre-modern communities, in that they are closed, or at least they guard their borders. My home is my castle. It is not just the community of the nation but, increasingly, all of Europe that is becoming just such a castle. *My family, my nation*: we look after the interests of our own families and our own nations; our relations with other nations are limited to tactical alliances formed to better secure those interests. This is what sociologists and social psychologists mean when they talk about the "amoral familism." We have no duties toward that which is not ours.

One might respond by pointing out the existence of another space, also a modern-day invention, but one that is conterminous with neither the family nor the nation: civil society. Nor is it just another word for the market, in the economic sense. In civil society, people operate as free individuals (free also from the constraints of family ties and national or ethnic affiliations) who associate for various purposes and are capable of undertaking concerted actions of various kinds. As true as this may be, the distinctness of civil society from the economic realm in particular has always posed a certain theoretical and practical problem. This is already apparent, at the theoretical level, in the writings of Hegel, for whom civil society is, above all else, the sphere of individual interests or needs and their satisfaction, which is only possible through mediation with the universal.[8] Not coincidentally, however, for Marx—who stripped the concept of its civic-civil core to reveal its bourgeois-economic character—the respectable citizen (*Bürger*, *citoyen*) in civil society (*bürgerliche Gesellschaft*) appeared disconcertingly similar to the regular bourgeois...One can find practical confirmation of the above by tracing the evolution, over the past decade, of non-governmental organizations. According to one increasingly popular view, NGOs, long the bedrock of civil society, have a tendency to transform into businesses—if not in the sense of entities that generate private profit, then at least in the manner in which they operate or the organizational structures they assume. Not to mention that, if we were to examine their role from a broader perspective, one can't help but get the impression that NGOs contribute to the onslaught of neoliberalism, meaning the systematic restriction of the social services provided by the state. The responsibility of providing these services, which one might want to finance with a progressive income tax, for example, is shifted onto the third sector, where social policy is carried out by volunteers, interns, and entry-level employees who are willing to work for low pay on precarious contracts. It's a solution that's brilliant in its simplicity. For this and other reasons, it is becoming increasingly hard to believe that civil society will save us from the unbridled forces of the market, or that new forms of common life will emerge from there, of all places.

In order for these to appear, we would need a space in which to experiment without being shackled by the logic of the market or limited to the confines of the family and national or cultural communities. One such space, in the 1960s, was the counterculture movement, whose reputation today isn't particularly good. Some blame counterculture for accelerating the decline of "traditional values" by bringing about the sexual revolution and women's liberation, while others see in it a fifth column or even a vanguard of capitalism, as it made household words out of terms like "creativity," which were then claimed by the managerial caste, many of whose members were former rebels moving on to a new, stable stage in their lives and were trying to put their radical slogans to use in the operations of private companies.[9] Both these critical approaches to counterculture overlook a few critical issues. Setting aside the question of whether so-called traditional values were worth defending, if examples of such values included the patriarchal domination of husbands over their wives, it is debatable whether a sexual revolution actually occurred. In any case, there is much evidence that the supposed revolution was immediately followed by a period of conservative backlash. Meanwhile, left-leaning critics who see the neoliberal model of management and employment as the fulfillment of countercultural demands (horizontal networks in place of former hierarchical structures, fluidity, mobility, people moving from one project to the next instead of finding lifelong employment) commit two other errors. First, they focus their critique on a narrow understanding of the economic sphere, on the counterculture's alleged role in the transformation of the capitalist economy. Second, and more importantly, they base their arguments on an either oversimplified or overly metaphysical model of social and historical causation. The fact that countercultural slogans were adopted and exploited by marketing gurus doesn't mean that the new spirit of capitalism simply grew out of the counterculture, or that there was a straightforward causal relationship between the two, much less that the former was, from the very beginning of the counterculture movement, its sole profound meaning. Someday, someone will write a history that does justice to the rebellion of the 1960s by portraying it as a revolt against the poverty of forms of living offered by modern capitalist society, particularly forms of common living. We smirk when we read or see the radicals of the time condemning the family as a "bourgeois superstition" and dressing up as Indians (what else are hippie clothes?) in order to emphasize their non-affiliation with the great nation or even the "white man's" culture. This aloofness toward the family and the concept of romantic love, as well as the mistrust of the community of the nation, nevertheless made possible experiments in the realm of common living, in comparison with which today's efforts seem completely stagnant. To be sure, these attempts weren't always successful, but anyone who today attempts to supersede the logic of the public sphere by developing a new logic of the common[10] would do well to keep them in mind and learn from them (and from their failures), if the commonwealth is in fact to be anchored in common living.

The greatest challenges facing not only the modern West, but perhaps global civilization in general — from economic inequalities to the looming specter of environmental catastrophe — are unlikely to be overcome without first answering the following question, or at least posing it as forcefully as possible: how are we to live together? The hypothesis, or perhaps the intuition, that I develop throughout the course of this essay can be summarized by stating that in order to develop new forms of common living, we must first revive the culture of friendship. The family, the community of the nation, and civil society are all, by themselves, insufficient to counterbalance the modern (or late-capitalist) anomie. Even though these three strictly modern forms continue to undergo radical transformations that render their futures unpredictable, it seems unlikely that they will produce, by the force of their own historical logic, solutions to the problems we face today. It is likely that families are possible without amoral familism, perhaps even nations without national egoism, and civicness untouched by the instrumentalizing forces of the market, but there must invariably appear an element external to the existing mode of functioning of the family, the nation, and civil society. The element, or rather the type of relationship that could destabilize them, thereby in a sense healing them, is friendship. However, we must attempt from the very beginning to think of friendship beyond the traditional opposition between the public and the private; instead of placing it within (fundamentally apolitical) spheres of private interpersonal relations, we must see it as having a certain quality or power to permeate relations of various types. From the philosophical standpoint, one of the most interesting characteristics of friendship is that while it is not synonymous with love, fraternity, or political alliance, none of these (or many other) relationships occur without a certain measure of friendship: this is the ingredient that makes other forms of relationships more productive and less limiting, less self-centered, and less toxic. Friendship is what enables us to breathe deeply, so to speak, preventing us from withdrawing into the logic of ingroup favoritism (our family, our nation, our culture, our interests). For this reason, to overcome the crisis of modern communities and societies, to solve the crisis facing modern forms of common living, we must return to the ethos of friendship and imbue with it our mutual relationships with other humans, and perhaps with other species.

What do we mean when we talk about "revival" or "return"? Do we suffer some lack of the culture or ethos of friendship? And if so—if our difficulty in inventing the indispensable new art of common living is in fact a sign of such a deficiency—then has there ever been a culture and an ethos, a golden age of friendship, which could serve as a model for us today? To answer this question, one would ultimately have to write something along the lines of a history of friendship, perhaps one similar to the histories written by Foucault. Interestingly, Michel Foucault himself, in an interview for the American LGBT magazine *The Advocate*, one of the last he gave before his death, stated outright: "One thing that interests me now is the problem of friendship...I think now, after studying the history of sex, we should try to understand the history of friendship, or friendships. That history is very, very important."[11] We can only regret that Foucault did not live long enough to accomplish his goal. All the more reason, therefore, to investigate the clues he left us in this interview and in an earlier conversation, significantly entitled "Friendship as a Way of Life." The latter interview was also published in a periodical targeted at a largely gay readership, this time in France. This is no coincidence; in this interview, Foucault expresses the conviction that "homosexuality," not by virtue of some essence or nature of homosexual "desire," but by its unique position within the social fabric, provokes questions about friendship as a way of life and, by extension, about "affective and relational virtualities."[12] The point is that homosexual relationships challenge the traditional model of the *couple*, and must by their very nature experiment with the very form of "being together": "How is it possible for men to be together? To live together, share their time, their meals, their room, their leisure, their grief, their knowledge, their confidences?"[13] Foucault contrasts this practice of building a relationship outside the traditional couple model with the stereotype of homosexual relationships as being inherently fleeting and too impermanent to permit the creation of any form of common living. It is between these two familiar molds—between the couple, the most established form of which is the modern, patriarchal, bourgeois married couple, and the absent or insufficient relationship that defines the random, anonymous encounter between two "men meeting in the street, seducing each other with a look, grabbing each other's asses and getting each other off in a quarter of an hour"[14]—that there unfolds a space for experimentation, but also for friendship, in the sense of a relationship that is unlike both romantic love and the indifferent collision of human atoms. One can of course argue whether Foucault is justified in granting special status to homosexual relationships in his discussion of the cultivation of friendships as a way of life, but his view is not an isolated one; Anthony Giddens also noted that new forms of intimate relationships are often developed today outside the boundaries of heteronormativity.[15] It's as if the exception to the rule were itself becoming the source of new, fluid rules that are gradually replacing the established models. Either way, both interviews from Foucault's later (latest) period of activity contain certain elements of a yet-unwritten history of friendship. The first of the two elements applies more to the present day than to history *per se*. In the case of friendship, its ethical potential—the one tied to its ethos, its way of being, and its capacity to create new ways to live together—is strictly tied to the difference between a friendship and a romantic relationship, upon which, ambivalence notwithstanding, the idea of the modern bourgeois family is based. The other element—which is mentioned later in the interview, and which Foucault does not associate directly with the former, despite the ostensible connection between the two—is the philosopher's recommendation that, in writing the future history of friendship, we pay particular attention to the point when, to put it colloquially, things started falling apart, when friendship, at least in "our" culture, began to be perceived as something insignificant, perhaps even as some sort of threat. Here Foucault once again raises the matter of homosexuality, noting that "once friendship disappeared as a culturally accepted relation, the issue arose: 'What is going on between men?'"[16] At first glance, this observation seems to run counter to his earlier point: he presents homosexuality not as a space for cultivating friendship, but as a problem (for normalizing power) precisely because of the "disappearance" or gradual recession of friendship from our horizon of experience. This contrast is superficial, however; in reality, these statements complement each other, and their common denominator is that they point to a certain absence. Friendship has "disappeared," and for this reason homosexual relations, which previously existed under its cover, became a problem, and have remained so to this day, albeit in a more positive, productive sense, thanks to attempts to rebuild the ethos and the culture of friendship within homosexual—or gay, to use a contemporary term much more appropriate to the context—relationships. This perspective raises a number of questions, ones similar to those Foucault himself asked when writing his existing, rather than prospective, histories. How did this disappearance begin, what historical forces prompted it, and what broader historical trends did it coincide with? What form did friendships take before that critical moment? Is this actually a matter of disappearance or recession, or was it simply the function of friendship that changed? To answer these questions, we would have to step outside Foucault and the remarks he makes in this interview—certainly an interesting and inspiring one, but whose observations are sketched in broad strokes. He naturally mentions antiquity as a period in which friendship was not only highly regarded by philosophers, but was above all granted particular social and economic significance. But in the very next sentence, he skips to the turn of the sixteenth and seventeenth centuries, at which point, he observes, there began to appear texts that "explicitly criticized friendship as something dangerous." Both indications are rather general, and while the view that *philia* was a significant feature of Greek life is a rather popular one, Foucault's placement of the collapse or breakdown of friendship culture in the late sixteenth century might seem arbitrary. Indeed, he lofts this hypothesis without any developed historical analysis to support it, implying simply that the collapse was tied to the way the army, state bureaucracies, and—most importantly—schools function. "I think there can be seen a very strong attempt in all these institutions to diminish or minimize the affectional relations," he says.[17] In places where this was particularly challenging, namely, in schools (run by Jesuits), the institution would simultaneously restrict and, to a certain extent, use these relations. These remarks bring to mind

Foucault's writings on later periods in history. In *Discipline and Punish*, his book on the birth of the disciplinary society at the turn of the eighteenth and nineteenth centuries, he portrays the school—along with the army, factory, and prison—as an institution of discipline and normalization, the success of which depends on significant restriction or regulation of horizontal relations between students, with the goal of supervision and exploitation. Just as the production process in a factory is detrimental to all fraternization among workers (private conversations, unscheduled breaks, etc.), institutionalized education does not benefit from intensely affective relations among students during recess, between classes, and in their free time spent together in the dormitory. It could be said that disciplinary power, in its ideal form, produces (produced?) the greatest possible affective dispersal of the individuals over which it is wielded, while simultaneously partitioning their concentration and motivation (to work, study, fight) through the normalizing gaze: each person in a separate cell, visible to the warden potentially or actually standing in a tower in the center of the panopticon.[18]

Does this mean that Foucault's proposed dividing line ought to be moved 200 years into the future? The analyses proposed by the French historian Anne Vincent-Buffault seems to suggest this. She also attempts to identify the turning point in the history of friendship, the moment in which its significance begins to wane in favor of other affective relations. Though the subtitle of her book suggests otherwise,[19] she bases her discussion less on the practices of friendship and more on the discourses about it, devoting particular attention to philosophical treatises. It is precisely at the beginning of the nineteenth century that Buffault observes an interesting process, namely, a precipitous drop in interest in friendship among authors who considered themselves philosophers and were regarded as such by the reading public. If the eighteenth century produced a veritable explosion of philosophical literature on the subject of friendship, not just learned treatises, but also a more popular variety of philosophy, the advice books of the period, then the next century witnessed a distinct turn toward other subjects. Buffault makes it clear that the disappearance of friendship from the horizon of pure philosophy and the adoption of the motif by poetry and literature is not necessarily synonymous with the disappearance or restriction of the practices themselves,[20] but she does connect the process to the growing role of family life, and married life in particular, with which the existing intense practices of friendship may clash. Strictly speaking, the conflict occurs to the degree in which the family, in the sense of the modern nuclear family, is to be the most important area of the individual's life outside the professional realm. With regard to the latter, "we often hear emphasized the challenges of reconciling ambition, rivalry, and competition with friendship,"[21] while outside the workplace, and as a sort of counterbalance to it, the family is treated as a realm in which married parents establish something of an affective monopoly, an exclusive right to the attention, concern, and selfless kindness of the partner. The friendly intimacy of the husband with another man, let alone another woman, threatens this monopoly and may be interpreted as a form of infidelity. This works both ways, however. If there existed in the eighteenth century a culturally sanctioned, or at least tolerated, phenomenon of female friendship with the capacity for more or less openly erotic elements,[22] then later centuries witnessed much more explicit pressure being placed on women to enter the confines of marital life, without the unnecessary, and potentially dangerous, remainder of affective friendship with members of the same sex. Friendship among women wasn't swept away by the nineteenth-century expansion of the patriarchal family model and the desire to control the sexuality and affective energy of women, but it did become suspect to men and husbands. It is no surprise, therefore, that philosophers—especially those who wrote advice books—

began to focus instead on problems encountered in married life and the family, shifting their attention away from the noble but increasingly irrelevant art of friendship.

Even during the expansion of the bourgeoisie, with its values and lifestyle, there existed a distinctive sphere in which friendship appeared to retain its rights. Strictly speaking, this was not so much a sphere as it was a period in the life of the individual, spanning childhood and adolescence. As he studied the history of the practices of the self and care of the self, Foucault took particular note of the moment at which these practices became— incompletely and conditionally—universal, in the sense that they became widespread in Greco-Roman culture, filtering down into the lower classes, and in the sense that cultivating the self was recognized as a necessary part of life at all its stages, from youth to old age. This, according to Foucault, was the "golden age" of the culture of the self in the first centuries of the common era.[23] In the case of early nineteenth-century friendship practices, precisely the opposite process took place, namely, the restriction of the scope of friendship culture, the delineation of narrow boundaries beyond which it becomes unnecessary, superfluous, or is seen as a sign of immaturity. Friendship is appropriate in childhood or adolescence, after which—if it continues with an affective charge and intensity that prevents it from being reduced to merely a useful or conventional "acquaintance"—it becomes an obstacle to the fulfillment of a person's professional and familial duties. What is more, as Foucault's observation about Jesuit schools makes clear, even within these narrow boundaries, friendship is simultaneously desirable and requires constant supervision. Buffault writes in this context about the contradiction between the view—increasingly popular among parents themselves—that friendship is an important part of growing up and integration into society, and the principle, espoused by educational institutions, of restricting interactions among their charges, especially when these contacts take the

16

form of unhealthy, affective relations that conflict with the goal of discipline.[24] Yet there is another contradiction to be seen here, one that erodes the institutions themselves: on the one hand, if discipline is to be effective, then individuals must be prevented from engaging in tight horizontal relations that could lead to offenses against morality, but also to rebellion, obstruction, etc.; on the other hand, these types of interactions can never be eliminated completely, and perhaps to do so would be undesirable. The school is a disciplinary institution, but it serves also the purpose of socialization, and rather than eliminate all manifestation of affective bonds between individuals, it might therefore be preferable to assume control of these relations, integrating them into the pedagogical process, thereby encouraging students to work more intensely and effectively (for example, by channeling them into study groups and peer tutoring).

It seems, therefore, that the crucial turning point in the history of friendship was the nineteenth century: the birth of modernity in the sense of an order that is politically post-revolutionary, culturally bourgeois, and, last but not least, economically and socially capitalistic. But to what can we compare this modern era? To the *ancien* régime directly preceding it? To ancient Greece? Has a golden age of friendship ever existed, for that matter? The sociologist Alois Hahn distinguishes three historical periods that he believes to be the high points of friendship culture: antiquity, the courtly noble world of seventeenth- and eighteenth-century France, and the years 1750–1850 in Germany.[25] The latter proposal indicates that we must consider the unique character of Germany, in particular German Romanticism. To what extent does this last element contradict the claim, made by Buffault and based on the French example, that friendship was suppressed by the bourgeois? Might it have something to do with Germany's "backwardness" in terms of developing a modern bourgeois society, or are there other factors at play here? These are just a couple of the questions that immediately come to mind. Ultimately, it would probably be best to abandon the desperate search for a model era in which friendship blossomed unimpeded, and instead sketch a more diverse portrait of the modern world itself, from which neither the practices nor the theories of friendship have ever disappeared completely. In other words: to think about different historical eras not in terms of a lost idea or, conversely, in terms of collapse, but to extract from them alternative means of problematizing and practicing friendship. One would then examine not just moments thus far considered to be high points of friendship culture, but also other periods in which it was ostensibly in retreat. So, for example, a separate study would be required of the story of friendship in early Christianity. Despite what one might think, Christianity, with its undoubted central focus on *agape*, or love, does not abandon the notion of friendship, but imbues it with a new interpretation, one anchored in, yet distinct from, its antique models. In fact, this has a basis in the Bible.[26] The question of friendship itself in the first centuries of Christianity is remarkably broad and has yet to be fully studied by historians.[27] The subject remains relevant in later periods; it resurfaces in the writings of Thomas Aquinas, and returns with even greater force in the Renaissance.[28] A separate challenge, finally, would be posed by the Greek or Greco-Roman chapter of this story, with its classical understanding of friendship, upon which nearly all later authors draw. In fact, even in ancient Greece alone, is there a single understanding of friendship to speak of? A cursory investigation of the word *philia* reveals an almost infinite multitude of connotations; it can refer to the most general principle of the universe, the harmonious coexistence of things (to the Pythagoreans or to Empedocles, and also later, to at least some of the Stoics), or to relations among people or even between just two individuals. It can be listed alongside love and *eros* or placed at the opposite pole. It can be instrumental or tangential to political relations. It can appear in the home and in relations between family members, or it can by definition exceed the boundaries of this realm.[29]

The problems posed by the richness and complexity of the historical material are compounded by theoretical, methodological, and hermeneutical difficulties. How do we write a history of friendship? Should it be primarily a history of a certain idea or concept and its shifting meanings, or rather a history of its actual practices? Likely the former and the latter, but balancing the ratio of both would be a difficult task, as would be determining the nature of the correlations between them. The theories of friendship and the treatises written about it are not faithful renditions of how, why, and for what reason people were friends across the centuries—or at least it would be hasty to assume as much. On the other hand, even in the case of theories divorced from social practice, the degree and especially the type of detachment are in themselves noteworthy. It is not insignificant, for example, who educates whom on the matter of friendship by suggesting role models, even if the latter are precisely that—role models, not descriptions of specific practices. At the same time, it seems that the history of friendship as an idea would be much easier to reconstruct, growing easier as its adopted understanding of friendship grew more abstract and philosophical. Philosophers, rarely skilled in historical or sociological methods, would certainly agree. The history of ideas is written in texts. And while most of our knowledge about historical practices is also based on texts, they are more dispersed and documentary, they require critical evaluation, and so on. When we consider these and other challenges, the task of the historian of ideas or concepts—or at least that of one who focuses mainly on concepts, treating practice as socio-historical background or context—may seem easier. And yet, even here, we will sooner or later have to face difficult questions, beginning with the fundamental matter of the identity or historical continuity of the very subject of the analysis. I mentioned above the understanding of friendship in Christian thought. Besides early Christian authors, one name that is frequently referenced in this context is that of Thomas Aquinas, particularly in relation to the treatise *De Caritate*. But does this give us grounds to claim that what Aquinas discusses in this treatise is *friendship*? Does *caritas* mean the same as *philia*? The title of the English edition of this minor work is translated as *On Charity*. The text itself naturally contains the words *amicitia* and *amicus*, but here, again, the matter is not quite as simple as that. To dismiss the problem by stating that different words with disparate etymologies and connotations, words belonging to different semantic fields (*amicitia* skews friendship slightly toward *amor*, which has echoes in the contemporary French word *ami*, a cognate of *amour*, but not in the English *friend* or German *Freund*) always refer to the exact same concept would be hermeneutically careless. On the other hand, despite these semantic shifts and inconsistencies, it would be equally hasty to conclude that a history of friendship cannot be written. We somehow sense that all these transformations and ruptures are still part of that very history, a history that runs from *philia* through *amicitia* to friendship, *amitié*, and *Freundschaft*, and beyond.

Some parts of the history of friendship in the West already exist, others have yet to be written. But this history needs to be lent philosophical heft, not necessarily — or at least not exclusively — by emphasizing the story of the idea or concept of friendship (and the milestones marked by the writings of Plato, Aristotle, Cicero, Cassian, Aquinas, Montaigne, Kant, Nietzsche, and Derrida), but more importantly by inscribing it into the logic of broader historical and cultural processes, and finally by meshing it with a philosophical reflection on the present. The following discussion takes that latter step, one that is more compatible with the essay format and does not require quite as broad and methodical research as would necessarily go into an exhaustive study of the complete history of the topic in all its philosophical, sociological, and psychological complexity. This leads us back to the problem of the crisis of modern forms of being together, and to the hypothesis that what we need in order to overcome it is a revival of the culture of friendship. Both the evaluation of the crisis and the hypothesis about the condition necessary (though certainly not sufficient) to overcome it require further elaboration, in which historical, as well as psychological and conceptual, analyses will play a role. In what areas is the scarcity of friendship culture most apparent today? As far as theory is concerned, with the gigantic volume of all types of research being carried out all over the world in countless academic and quasi-academic institutions, it's hard to argue that any subject has been neglected or completely forgotten. Friendship is certainly the subject of some writing and discussion today, including in the context of the challenges facing the modern world. To claim that we are witnessing some clear renaissance of this issue, however, would be premature. Even if their general premises are correct, not all analyses of this type are fruitful or particularly interesting from the philosophical point of view. We must therefore persist in these efforts; this essay is just such an attempt to approach, to draw closer to the subject of friendship. Its two main axes are plotted by the initial observation that, on the practical plane, the forms of community promoted by modernity as a counterweight to its own alienated model of association are marked by a lack or deficit of friendship—or, more specifically, the observation that this promotion is a sign that friendship culture is in retreat. The discussion therefore addresses the subject of the modern family: not just the family itself, but also—and more broadly—our understanding of love and the transformations under way in our intimate relations. How does friendship fit into them, currently and potentially? The other set of issues that is discussed in relation to the question of friendship revolves around politics.

Not that the family, marriage, love, or intimate relations are by their very nature apolitical; they are quite obviously permeated by myriad power relations, and the conflicts, acts of resistance, and compromises that occur within them directly affect the scope and types of freedom available to us. Along with our small family communities, however, the modern world grants us membership of a larger national community, which points to politics in a more direct, and in essence perhaps in a more traditional and almost archaic, sense of the word. The following analyses center not so much on the nation or nation state as a category, but on the ingroup logic that governs every variety of nationalism as well as today's discourse of cultural conflict: on the absolute Schmittian binary of the ingroup, our friends, and the outgroup, or our enemies. Is it possible to consider friendship outside of this dichotomous mold? The choice of these two areas or types of issues is of course limiting and somewhat arbitrary, but it seems to be at least partially justified by the increasingly widespread feeling that it has become particularly difficult to live together, first, as men and women in various social and intimate configurations, and second, as global citizens confronting the increasingly real specter of the return or emergence of new forms of fascism.

Chapter 2

Just Friends?

It is not a lack of love, but a lack of friendship that makes unhappy marriages.
F. Nietzsche, Nachlass (1876)

Nearly all philosophers who have written about love, including the Greeks, have had something to say about the relationship between friendship and love. Not that any of them ever succeeded in fully explaining the issue or even proposing some accepted and precise way of distinguishing between the two. Even Plato, in the *Lysis*, his dialog on *philia* and *philein*, uses these words interchangeably with *epithymia, epithymein, eros, eran,* and *agapan*. This doesn't change the fact that the author of the *Laws*, and the ancient thinkers who succeeded him, consistently returned to the question about the ties between friendship and love—real ties, despite the differences between them. We owe to these philosophers a few characteristic and oft-repeated motifs. Most importantly, unlike friendship, which seems to be a stable relation, a *longue durée* phenomenon (at least in the scale of human life), love erupts in a sudden burst and quickly fizzles out. As Aristotle says, "Now it looks as if love were a feeling, friendship a state of character."[1] And that is why the latter ought to be the goal of the former. Love is valuable insofar as it tends toward stabilization in friendship.[2] But there are other issues involved with the passionate nature of love. Not only is it less permanent or stable than friendship, it is also related, in a sense, to madness. For this reason it seems, at first glance, inferior to the rational *philia*. The suspicion that passionate love is something like an illness that we must all eventually catch, but from which we must be cured, as it can prove fatal, must have been widespread in Plato's day, since he mentions it in Lysias' speech in *The Phaedrus*.[3] Love blinds us and deprives us of our reason; what is worse, it can persuade even the best person to act dishonorably. A friend, meanwhile—at least so it is claimed by those authors who held in highest regard the form of friendship that occurred "between the good"[4] (many of them, at least in antiquity)—cannot be expected to perform a dishonorable, ignoble, or petty act. That would contradict the very essence of friendship. On the other hand, the Greeks believed that certain kinds of rage, mania, and inspiration could be valid sources of metaphysical insight.[5]

It's tempting to say, with certain reservations, that the Greeks valued friendship more than love—unlike us, modern people, with our peculiar cult of love, and our willingness to grant friendship full rights only in the realm of childhood and youth. But such a depiction would be more than an oversimplification: it would also be anachronistic, and not just because of the way our understanding of friendship has changed throughout our culture's history. The modern meaning of love is also completely different from that of the ancient world. Our use of this particular word to convey the meaning of the Greek *eros* can be highly misleading. To claim that, between Greek antiquity and modern times, a reversal of hierarchies has taken place within the same relation of love and friendship, would be to assume that the terms of that relation have remained unchanged, or in any case have changed only insignificantly. And yet Greek erotics, as we ought to refer to matters associated with *eros*, has little in common both with our understanding of erotics and with the familiar idea of romantic love. If Foucault is correct in his analysis, then it belongs, on the one hand, to the realm of *aphrodisia*, or "contacts that produce a certain form of pleasure"[6] (which brings it close to the "art of love," in the sense of *art erotica*), and on the other hand it is inscribed in the divisions and differences in rank and status among free citizens (which points to the central problem in Greek erotics, namely, the passivity of the seduced youth vis-à-vis the older, or at any rate mature, man who seduces him; passivity conflicts with freedom, which is why the former must be delineated, ritualized, coded, etc.[7]). Because of this second aspect, erotics applies fundamentally to male-male relations. Of course, relations between men and women, particularly between spouses, were not beyond the horizon of reflection in antiquity, but their place was elsewhere: they belonged to economics, the everyday matters of the household. Emotional relations were also part of these economics insofar as they contributed to peace and harmony within the home, and to the general well-being of the family. It is only later that they acquired an autonomous meaning. Meanwhile, we modern people, Foucault argues, have lost all sense of *ars erotica* and have replaced erotics with sexuality, or rather with the mystery of desire, which demands constant exploration and is a source of fascination and fear, and without which the "dispositive of sexuality" could not operate. Even erotics in the service of transgression (in the Bataillian sense) has less to do with the body and pleasure and more to do with desire (and its relation to the law). It is this new realm, the realm of desire, that gives rise to the contemporary form of love. To understand the ratio between love and friendship today, we must first closely examine the former of the two. So thoroughly has love dominated our intimate relations that only a narrow margin is left for friendship, which has largely been relegated to the role of a salve for the pains and disappoints of our love lives.

What we call romantic love may appear to have little in common with the idea of the stable, bourgeois family or even with the couple, the spread of which was to marginalize relationships founded on friendship. On the one hand we have the poetry of passion, and on the other—the prose of married or quasi-married life. It is no coincidence that when romantic love stories culminate in the happy union of lovers, they end at the moment when they go on to "live happily ever after." Reality is much more complicated. What we actually witness is a certain tension and ambivalence. The common thread between romantic elation and the bourgeois household isn't just the fact that the former is a constitutive condition of the latter. The shared roots run much deeper and are tied to the aforementioned logic of desire that has superseded the erotics of antiquity. Desire is no longer first and foremost, or perhaps even at all, the desire for sensual pleasure (*aphrodisia*). Furthermore, it functions in a social realm that is completely different from the one in which the Greek *eros* circulated; it is no longer a *polis*, a space of encounters among free and equal people (men), but a modern society based on market competition and the nuclear family. The latter doesn't simply constitute the ultimate aim of love, it imposes upon it its own code, as the place in which desire is enclosed (even if this is never completely successful). As we said above, love—in its modern incarnation—is the basic form of desire. We must keep in mind, however, that desire, as Lacan says, is always the desire of the Other (*désir de l'Autre*). This has certain consequences. As Lacan argues, this Other is more than just the object toward which our desire is directed (its *genetivus objectivus* sense), but also—at a deeper level—the object that desires in us, the true subject of our desire (*genetivus subjectivus*). We desire the Other, but our desire is subject to certain laws; it is in a sense structured, encoded by what Lacan calls the "symbolic order." My intention here is not to explore the many complexities of the theories of Freud and Lacan. What is relevant—perhaps not in the clinical sense, but in line with basic psychoanalytical intuitions—is that the objective determinants of desire make it more or less *neurotic*, that is, they mark it with anxiety and a sort of compulsivity.[8] As desiring beings, we are all neurotic to a certain extent. The question of whether the neurotic mark on desire is universal in its scope is a matter for a separate discussion, but even the most obstinate opponents of this claim, such as Deleuze and Guattari, admit that the process of neuroticization, though it contradicts the schizophrenic nature of desire, is quite real indeed.[9] Though not every personality is neurotic, the personality of our time certainly is.

In that case, is romantic love a form of neurosis? This may sound like a very negative and reductionist diagnosis, yet practically every aspect of neurosis is something we typically think of as something that "sublimates" our understanding of love. First, though passionate love will always be stigmatized, to some degree at least, as fleeting and impermanent, and though the "desire of the Other" implies that it will never be satisfied with the Same, this desire is nevertheless bound by the figure of "the One" (if *she's* not the One, then it must be someone else). This, in turn, constitutes a neuroticizing effect of Oedipus: the original object of one's desire is the mother. You only have one mother, as the platitude goes, and for this reason, though there are many possible objects of desire, though they form a multitude, they are essentially placeholders standing in for that one object, the One. It is this oedipal fixation that is responsible for the Romantic notion (albeit one with counterparts reaching back into antiquity) of the "other half" that is somewhere out there, waiting for us. This is an interpretation one might arrive at from the perspective of Freudian theory, which focuses on the male subject and male desire.[10] The same applies to the frustration caused by the repression and displacement of libido within the oedipal triangle. Is it not here that we find the source of the lofty notion that loving desire is infinite and effectively insatiable, that it is eternal hunger or yearning? And, finally, the resolution of the oedipal situation, both in the Freudian sense (identification with the father) and in the Lacanian sense (the internalization of the symbolic order represented by the Name of the Father), is not without effect on our romantic relations and lends them extraordinary significance; from this point on, what is at stake in our search for the Other is, effectively, our identity and how well we live up to the gender and social roles we perform. This evokes fear, but modern love would not be what it is without that fear and without that incessant anxiety.

What is the place and role of friendship in a world in which the desires of men and women are channeled mainly toward finding the One, in order to fulfill the expectations of the symbolic Father and to assuage their neurotic fears? Besides the aforementioned purpose of socializing the individual in peer groups during childhood and adolescence, it undoubtedly serves other roles in adulthood. At that stage, however, friendship becomes intertwined with that fundamental human drive. First, a friend can be a confidant in matters of the heart. This is a stereotypical view of female friendships and the role of the girlfriend.[11] Is he the One? If he is, then how do I get him and hold on to him? Questions of this type emerge during the stage of romantic pursuit and maneuvering. These matters cannot be discussed with the potential or current object of one's affections, for obvious reasons. Some third party is therefore necessary, some confidant or confidante to whom we can divulge our doubts, desires, and so on. That same person (or someone who serves the same function) often accompanies us through the later stages of the romantic relationship, whether it is that of stabilization or—equally likely—bitter disappointment. When the One turns out to be "just like all the others," or even worse, we inevitably seek comfort again in the confidante (or the confidant, if *having* the One female turns out to be less attractive than *desiring* her). Second, friendship can itself assume the form of a romantic relationship, and function in a similar way. The friend then becomes the One, with all the attendant consequences, including jealousy, fear of abandonment, idealization (and the inevitable risk of disappointment), and ambivalent emotions ranging from boundless devotion to secret antipathy. The roles of these two types of friends, the confidant and the beloved friend, can, of course, be played by the same person; in the case of heterosexual relationships, it is typically a person of the same sex. Whenever friendship competes with love in this manner (in a sense playing the same game), it is safer for a man to consult with a male friend and for a woman to confide in a girlfriend, lest their intimate friendship with the Other provoke open conflict. This is one possible meaning of the oft-expressed belief that "men and women can never just be friends." This is less a consequence of some aspect of male or female nature (particularly the erotic tension between the two, as if *eros* were inherently incompatible with friendship), and more a result of the order into which men and women are plunged by the neuroticization of desire. Third, and finally, there also exists a form of friendship that is openly antagonistic toward romantic love between couples. The common stereotype, in this instance, is that such bonds occur among groups of men. At any rate, it can be said that in the case of men, a relationship of this type leads to the formation of a particularly ominous form of community based on hierarchy and cemented by outward and inward violence. Perhaps the male soldier or warrior type, one whom Klaus Theweleit describes as the fundamental psychophysical premise of fascism, is transhistorical and transcultural, as is male friendship understood and practiced as a community based on combat— or, more specifically, on killing. The Homeric sense of the word *philia* isn't free of such connotations and associations with brothers in arms, *philoi hetairoi*.[12] In any case, it appears that, in modernity, this male drive to assemble into warlike groups is inextricable from the desire encapsulated in the oedipal triangle. The family cannot be the be all and end all. A person must make every effort to leave the home and seek other stimuli outside the family. Women certainly sense this urge as well, but in a patriarchal society, their capacity to satisfy it is limited. When and because women stay at home with the children, men can leave the family space to meet other men and compete with them in the economic game. Yet the latter offers most of them little more than toil and frustration; it is not a true, positive counterweight to the frustration caused by the "double binds" of family life. Instead, it heaps on even more of them. At home the man, as the One, must be *both* a strong conqueror *and* a predictable (if not submissive) partner; at work, he must *both* obediently perform his duties *and* be a bold, creative entrepreneur of the self. Under such circumstances, he has but one choice. Or two, in fact, but the first—complete submission—is, under patriarchy, a complete contradiction of male agency. He therefore chooses the other option, namely, to join a community of men in which the rule of force is both absolute and explicit, and where he is no longer compelled to navigate conflicting demands. To be sure, a military unit, street gang, or a band of soccer hooligans will demand discipline and obedience from its members, but at the same time, bound by this peculiar form of brotherly friendship, they are permitted or even encouraged to perform open acts of violence as an expression of group unity.[13]

A confiding ear in matters of the heart, friendship that mimics romance, a community bound by combat: this is by no means an exhaustive list of modern and contemporary forms of friendship. They can, however, be treated as its characteristic forms. Their common feature is that they appear in a space dominated by the notion of romantic love and, each in their own way, complement it or compensate for its attendant anxieties—in the same way that others compensate, for example, for the absence of social trust and social solidarity (a friend is "someone you can always count on"). The question immediately arises: what could friendship be, what could it become, if our desire were to be reconfigured, if it were at least partially deneuroticized and deoedipalized? And would this process necessarily involve the reinforcement, within romantic relationships, of that which is associated with friendship? And prior to that: is neurosis really our destiny, and are love and desire themselves doomed to circulate in a vicious circle of oedipal fantasms? A close reading of Freud and Lacan would inevitably demonstrate that "love as a kind of neurosis" is only one possibility, one of many potential pathways for our libidos. This has been explored more emphatically by less orthodox psychoanalysts who, though they perceived neurosis to be a mass phenomenon, also recognized it to be the effect of specific mechanisms and social processes. Let us examine here a few of their observations and diagnoses.

Psychoanalytic revisionism, it seems, has shared the fate of the same counterculture upon which it once left a great mark. We think of ourselves as being much more "advanced" than Erich Fromm and Karen Horney, to the extent that the very mention of these names in psychoanalysis and social theory circles draws suspicion or, at best, pitying smiles. Such responses are certainly not unwarranted. Many of the solutions proposed by the above authors verge on the naïve and fanciful. However, as far as the fundamental critical-diagnostic aspect of their work is concerned, their analyses are only slightly outdated. Whatever we may say about the "narcissistic" personality of the Facebook generation, good old neurosis is holding up—or rather, it's holding us firmly in its strong embrace. The same is true of the possession-based model of relations with the world and with others. In this sense, the justified desire to move forward should entail the development, rather than the abandonment, of the issues addressed by the revisionists. Neopsychoanalysis leaves few illusions about love as it is manifested in contemporary society, To Fromm, love "in the mode of having it," love that is "confining, imprisoning, or controlling the object one loves," love that is "strangling, deadening, suffocating, killing" is in fact an absence of true love, and to call it love "is mostly a misuse of the word."[14] True love lets the other be; it is not dominating, jealous, or possessive. At the same time, Fromm states bluntly that, in his view, "loving [couples] are the exception rather than the rule."[15] In the end, it's not a matter of how we use the word "love," after all, but why our intimate relationships become so toxic. Here, again, we could say that despite their lack of an elaborate conceptual apparatus such as that developed by the Lacanian school, American revisionists have proven to be remarkably realistic in their analyses. Rather than stumble into the mysticism of constant lack, they point to the societal causes of this predicament. This theme is also emphasized in the writings of Horney, who explores more deeply the mechanism of neurotic love itself. She doesn't attribute it to possessiveness or, as she calls it, greediness *per se* (seeing it rather as an effect or symptom), but to *anxiety*.[16] It is *anxiety* that makes neurotic love possessive and, more importantly, compulsive. "Whenever a person is driven by strong anxiety, the result is necessarily a loss of spontaneity and flexibility. In simple terms this means that to a neurotic the gaining of affection is not a luxury, nor primarily a source of additional strength or pleasure, but a vital necessity."[17] Like Fromm, Horney does not reject love entirely, only a particular form thereof that she considers dominating. Compulsion and coercion have the effect, first, that we long to be loved, rather than to love. Second, we desire this not as something that gives our lives more intensity, but as a form of relief. The relief it offers is essential to our survival. The difference between these two moduses of love is not always easily perceptible at the empirical level, as it applies less to behavior and actions themselves, and more to their psychosomatic foundation. Whether jealously or the desire for the other's presence and attention constitute an expression of "healthy" love or a sign of neurotic anxiety need not be immediately apparent in words and gestures—or rather, it only becomes visible to the trained analytical eye and audible to ears attuned to what remains unsaid. One of the symptoms of neurosis is a deeply hidden but occasionally revealed antipathy to the object of one's love. "On the one hand, the neurotic seeks the other's interest and presence, fears to be disliked and feels neglected if the other is not around; and on the other, he is not at all happy when he is with his idol. If he ever becomes conscious of this contradiction he is usually perplexed about it."[18] Unlike

Lacanians, Horney demonstrates that neurotic love has little in common with idealization and idolization of the object of love as someone who is in possession of the *objet petite a*, etc. Here this fixation assumes the form of an ambivalent yet compulsive kind of clinging, more akin to dependence than to obsession. It's also significant that this neurotic anxiety leads to an impasse, a blockage of the energy of desire, but that this does not stem from the nature of the latter. It is not entirely explained by the Oedipus complex, understood as an invariant, a necessary and crucial stage of the libido's development, nor by any other structural feature or constellation of desire. It is debatable whether Horney's explanation of the sources of this anxiety are satisfactory, but she does point us in the right direction:

> Modern culture is economically based on the principle of individual competition. The isolated individual has to fight with other individuals of the same group, has to surpass them and, frequently, thrust them aside. The advantage of the one is frequently the disadvantage of the other. The psychic result of this situation is a diffuse hostile tension between individuals. Everyone is the real or potential competitor of everyone else.[19]

Anxiety is a consequence of this "diffuse hostile tension." Oedipus is relevant here only inasmuch as identifying with one of the parental figures or entry into the symbolic order signifies one's induction into the social space of competition: Will I ever be equal to my mother/father? Do I deserve their love? Do I even deserve to be loved? In this manner love, rather than providing a counterweight to the ubiquitous logic of competition, is itself marked or even shaped by it.

The analyses carried out by psychoanalytic revisionists rarely led them to revolutionary conclusions; what they called for, at most, was a "revolution of hope." This was not the case with Wilhelm Reich, who aspired to combine the call for social and sexual revolution. He, too, concluded that "neuroses have become a problem of the masses,"[20] and, like Fromm and Horney, believed that its roots lay in social reality. At the same time, Reich attached much greater importance to repression, perceiving it to be the key mechanism driving compulsive behavior, including the neurotic need for love. For this reason, he offers a different critique of the modern model of the couple, particularly the married couple. He constantly revisits in it two issues that are distinct but connected through the concept of repression: adolescent sexuality and monogamy. While other authors saw the fundamental problem of married life to be the neurotic character of love and the deficit of true, mature love in the mode of being, as Fromm would say, for Reich the problem was that the very institution of monogamous marriage was based on repression. Referring to the difference between desire and drive, we could say that he was interested not in curing the former, but in liberating the latter. And yet, in *The Sexual Revolution*, in which Reich explains his views with extraordinary precision, this project encounters substantial obstacles. At first glance, the nature of the problem seems almost mechanical—unbridled libidinal energy must either tear apart the constrictions of monogamy, or it must by repressed, inevitably leading to neurosis and unhappiness: "Since it is unlikely—sex-economically impossible—that someone who leads a completely gratifying sexual life will subject himself to the conditions of marital morality (only one partner, for life), the first requirement is a deep-seated repression of sexual needs, particularly in the woman."[21] In fact, this deep-seated repression begins earlier, in puberty, and therefore submitting to the rigors of married life requires little actual submission: from the very start, their sexual lives are not "completely gratifying." Reich appears to take a truly revolutionary stance in opposition to marriage and the family, and against "sex reformers" who attempt to salvage the former by subjecting it to "eroticization."[22] For this reason, he finds the Russian revolution to be a particularly interesting case, in which the release of the repressed natural needs of the people was initially met with political will on the part of the leaders, who hoped to achieve far-reaching sexual liberalization. Over several pages, Reich describes in great detail Soviet attempts to create new forms of common living in worker communes, where marriage and the family were approached as open issues that demanded solutions worthy of the new, revolutionary times. "They talked about 'family,'" he sneers, "and meant sexuality."[23] But the era of radical sexual politics quickly came to an end. Before it had even gotten well under way, the authorities performed a complete turnaround, restricting abortion, recriminalizing homosexuality, and reverting to the idea of the healthy (in this case: proletarian) family, while all experiments with free love were decried as "bourgeois" practices. The cause of this about-face wasn't just the immanent logic of the revolution, whose momentum gradually dissipates or gives way to *Realpolitik*, forcing the reinstatement, in some areas, of the previous order, though this was certainly one of the mechanisms at play. (It is somehow unsurprising that the first cause to be sacrificed by radicals in pursuit of other, more important, goals happened to be that of morality.) Reich finds a deeper and more distant, so to speak, cause for the failure of the Russian sexual revolution. It is deeper because it refers us to hidden psychic structures that cannot be transformed by an act of the political will. It is distant because those same structures are a product of "thousands of years [of] corrupt sexual morality."[24] Contemporary man is not ready for a sexual revolution. This is also apparent in the misguided—or at best woefully insufficient, in Reich's view— forms of sexual liberation that appear whenever it is carried out under existing circumstances (that is, without changing the deeper, psychophysical determinants).[25] Although the author of *The Function of the Orgasm* never attacks promiscuity *per se*, much less dismisses it as "bourgeois," parroting the conservative claim, he does describe it as "casual, loveless, and unsatisfying." Reich contrasts both loveless promiscuity and monogamous marriage with something he calls an "enduring sexual relationship," the endurance of which would be quantified not by its duration nor by the number of partners, but by a "concrete affirmation of man's sexual happiness."[26] One could point out that such happiness is not human nature; that same human nature, after all, that demanded its rights and rebelled against the plans of the revolutionaries and their dream of creating a "New Man." Countering this argument, Reich cites a figure that is hard to place clearly within the realm of either history or myth: namely, clan societies, which were structured by primitive communism and matriarchy, and whose members enjoyed unrestricted sexual freedom. The turning point in the history of humankind, he writes, was the transition from this form of social organization to a patriarchal society built on the institution of the family.

> The chieftain of the matriarchal clan organization, who originally was not in opposition to the clan society, gradually becomes the patriarch of the family, achieves an economic predominance, and develops progressively into the patriarch of the whole clan...The first classes were the family of the chieftain on the one hand and the *gens* (clan) on the other...The emerging "family man" begins to reproduce the increasingly patriarchal class organization of society by changing its own structure. The basic mechanism of this reproduction is the shift from sex affirmation to sex suppression; its basis is the dominating economic position of the chieftain.[27]

Thus, in the darkness of prehistory, the patriarchy, class divisions, and sexual repression are born concurrently...

Following this extended digression on the subject of romantic love, the associations between love and neurosis, and the intricacies of politics and the sexual revolution, it is time to return to the question of friendship. In our efforts to at least partially deneuroticize romantic relations, should we not seek to reinforce, within these relations themselves, the affects that are characteristic of friendship? And how do we identify those affects? The fact that the greatest philosophical minds have always struggled to clearly separate and distinguish between friendship and love is no mere accident. When observed in actual interpersonal relations, the two mix together, losing their clearly defined contours. There nevertheless appear to be certain features that are characteristic of friendship but whose presence is definitely weaker in love, and especially in neurotic or compulsive love. This applies in particular to compulsivity itself. Although Aristotle states that friendship "is one of the most indispensable requirements of life,"[28] he interprets this requirement in a rather peculiar way. He isn't thinking of the sort of "existential" necessity whose satisfaction is a condition for survival. Friendship is essentially a luxury; it is needed even by "rich men, rulers and potentates." What for? According to Aristotle, the ultimate meaning of friendship is virtue or the exercise thereof, as it gives us the ability to "assist [others] in noble deeds."[29] This argument echoes the philosopher's deliberations on the genesis of the state in *Politics*. According to an oft-cited dictum by Aristotle, while the state "comes into existence for the sake of life, it exists for the good life."[30] While the family exists to guarantee the survival of its members and the reproduction of the species, and is thus subject to the law of necessity, the *polis* rises above this rudimentary level. It is true that the state is formed by a community of "several villages," themselves a combination of "several households,"[31] but the meaning of its existence cannot be reduced to ensure the survival of individuals or the human race. Its purpose or meaning is for that life to be good. The author of the cited words (unlike some of his contemporary commentators) did not see this to be a radical break or even a discontinuity: Aristotle presented both the *polis* and the *oikois* as consistent with "nature" in the broadest sense of the word. He was certain to emphasize, however, the difference between the order of necessities tied to survival and the order of the good life, which is served by the political community. The good life is the purpose (*telos*) of a truly human life, but it also imbues it with a new, ethical quality. The same is true of friendship. It rises above the level of actions that are geared solely toward amassing and preserving wealth, power, and prestige. Right after he observes that friendship encourages ethical actions, without which all prosperity in the everyday sense (what "rich men, rulers and potentates" have) is nothing, Aristotle adds: "And how could such prosperity be safeguarded and preserved without friends?"[32] Still, friendship is essentially a kind of excess or surplus. This view finds its expression in the distinction—introduced in the *Nicomachean Ethics*—of three kinds or types of friendship, only one of which fully merits the term, or can at least be described as the superior, more perfect one. The first two kinds of friendship are based on utility and pleasure, respectively. The friendship that is more perfect than the other two occurs among "good men" who do not seek either thing (pleasure or utility), but only "each other."[33] It is a special predisposition that leads one to forge with another person an intimate bond whose only rationale is expressed in the simple statement: "Because it was him; because it was me."[34]

In what sense can this understanding of friendship be contrasted with romantic love? Does the concept of love not contain that same suspension of one's pursuit of utility, that same treatment of the other as a person? Doesn't its selflessness exceed that of friendship? So it would appear, in theory, but we must keep in mind the observations practicing analysts have made about the mundane reality of romantic relationships in the modern world. Their compulsive nature makes love much less selfless than it wishes to appear. However, the problem doesn't lie in utility in the narrow, material, or economic sense of the word (at least not with regard to compulsion), but in the coercion and obligation that burden it. Love is supposed to free us from anxiety, at least partially and momentarily. And in this sense, it is selfish; the other is ultimately the means rather than the end. In extreme cases, when love takes the form of real dependence, even to the extent of abnegating one's own goals and aspirations, it can be used as a kind of emotional blackmail, a way of tying down the partner ("See, I've sacrificed so much for you!"). Authors who write about friendship—with the exception of some Christian thinkers—rarely emphasize this aspect of self-sacrifice. To be sure, there is nothing true friends would not be ready to sacrifice for the sake of friendship. As Plato said, citing a view prevalent in his time, "All things are common among friends."[35] But this has nothing to do with the insincere self-sacrifice of romantic love. That is the last thing one could demand of a friend. After all, as we learned from Montaigne, a friend is supposed to be himself; friendship is about letting him be, about nurturing his autonomy. It could be said, therefore, that friendship blossoms wherever neurotic anxiety and its attendant compulsion wane. Furthermore, friendship differs from love inasmuch as romantic relations are marked by compulsion, just as the logic of excess differs from the logic of lack. If this is the nature of *true* (deneuroticized) love, then we would have to conclude that real love becomes true love insofar as it comes to resemble friendship.

Another unique quality of friendship—one partly associated with this lack of compulsion, this cleansing of anxiety, need, and lack—is that it is based on distance. This is yet another quality that sets it apart from love—both its real and ideal versions, it seems. If an important component of the idea of romantic love is the notion of melding, communion, becoming One with the object of our feelings, and if there is a clearly defined element of "bonding" in the practice of compulsive neurotic love, a forced symbiosis in response to the anxiety that marks our individual existence (that very symbiosis that leads innumerable men and women to utter, on their psychoanalyst's or therapist's couch, the ritual phrase about "feeling suffocated" in their relationship), then friendship is about respecting each other's boundaries and autonomy. Or at least about carefully maintaining a balance between an engulfing intimacy and withdrawal. In *The Metaphysics of Morals*, in a passage about friendship, Kant defines it as "the union of two persons through equal mutual love and respect."[36] He then combines love and attraction, stressing that excessive intimacy can ruin a friendship, and that one must therefore seek to strengthen the element of respect, which he likens to "repulsion."[37] Naturally, respect that is completely bereft of love's attraction is also insufficient; such a relation, Kant writes, would lack trust and resemble formal interactions between unequals. Like the interaction between a teacher and a pupil, they are characterized by respect, but are not necessarily friendships. Meanwhile, Barthes, in his discussion of the "phantasm of idiorhythmy," explains that what he has in mind is "something like solitude with regular interruptions: the paradox, the contradiction, the aporia of bringing distances together."[38] This cautious approach to communion and apprehension about being engulfed by the other or others is stated even more explicitly here than it is in Kant's concept of respect.[39] Paradoxically, it is this ("regularly interrupted") solitude that is to serve as the basis for our being or living together. Not coincidentally, Barthes is interested in a very particular type of community: a group in which "cohabitation does not preclude individual freedom";[40] not engulfing communities that offer a sense of security or belonging in exchange for one's autonomy, but groups based on autonomous coexistence. The true challenge is to devise a form of that latter that would nevertheless remain a form of cohabitation, rather than an alienated, indifferent existence beside each other. This appears to be the point in which Barthes could connect his "idiorhythmy" and friendship. Friendships, as the ancients said, live together, but that community (*koinonia*) is not synonymous with the loss of one's boundaries, much less with toxic symbiosis.

Both of these aspects of friendship—namely, the absence of compulsion and the distance upon which it is based—distinguish it from neurotic love. What is more, insofar as love itself exceeds the logics of lack, necessity, and coping with anxiety, it draws on friendship or contains it as an important constituent, alongside the erotic element, for example. This is not to say that the other constituents are attributed exclusively to romantic relationships. When we speak of "friendship" or "love," we don't refer to two distinct essences, but to nexuses and intersections of various elements and aspects that appear in varying proportions and move among these nexuses. In any case, it seems that our goal should be to transform our intimate relations into something that contains less compulsive anxiety and more mutual recognition of our autonomy. It is only where anxiety reigns that autonomy is interpreted as a kind of separateness that threatens with indifference. This kind of transformation cannot be carried out by decree. On the other hand, without it there will never be a sexual revolution worthy of the name. Even if Western societies, broadly speaking, have witnessed a loosening of the moral restrictions around sexuality since the mid-twentieth century, we are still light years away from Reich's utopia of "sexual happiness."

Reich's proposed *longue durée* perspective on the psychophysical structures hindering sexual liberation is informative, and doubly so. First, like any historical perspective, it depicts contemporary practices (monogamous marriage, bourgeois couples) as appurtenances of a particular form of society. There is nothing to indicate that these practices are the final word of the human race on how individuals should engage in intimate relations, what kinds of families they should live in, what parental configurations they should raise their children in, and what role the erotic should play in these configurations and relations. Even if the vision of primitive sexual communism or a matriarchal clan society preceding the birth of the patriarchy can be challenged on scientific grounds, one cannot but notice that humankind has employed myriad solutions with regard to the form of the family and its place within the broader social landscape, and that we can expect them to be equally varied in the future (assuming, that is, that the human race survives more than a dozen or so generations into the future). Second—and this is perhaps the more important lesson here—Reich himself demonstrates just how slow and difficult such changes are. Meanwhile, that is, while we try to live together, if we want to do more than just fantasize about living in some faraway era (one that belongs to prehistory or awaits our remote descendants), we essentially have no choice but to draw on established yet contingent forms of coexistence. Does this necessarily lead to passivity and fatalism in practice? Perhaps in reality there is no such thing as a fully "established" practice, as testified by today's widely observed crisis of the family and the couple. Contrary to what defenders of traditional models may claim, the crisis lies not in their disintegration—unless by disintegration we mean the negotiable character of these relations becoming apparent to individuals and in turn influencing their mutual relations. In this sense, the crisis is a thoroughly positive development. It is hard to tell, of course, whether some sort of turning point will be reached, some lasting transformation of our habitus. But we should not underestimate the positive significance of the ongoing redefinitions in the realm of intimate interpersonal relations. Anthony Giddens was among the first to observe them in his book *The Transformation of Intimacy*,[41] published in the early 1990s, in which he uses, with good reason, an idiom that is very well suited to a description of friendship. Giddens explicitly mentions friendship in only a few places, for example when he analyzes the weakening of male comradeship in the Victorian period, its relegation "to marginal activities, like sport or other leisure pursuits," while friendships between women, conversely, grew more intense, helping "mitigate the disappointments of marriage."[42] But what is this model that he calls "the pure relationship," which is gradually superseding romantic love as the dominant code of intimate relations, based on? The purification of intimate relations, Giddens argues, began with the appearance of romantic love, which separated love between individuals from economic determinants (at least to the extent in which a "marriage of love" was no longer a covenant between families of a particular status, income, etc.) What was an even more significant factor, however, was the later economic emancipation of women and their entrance into the labor market (even if they had yet to achieve equal standing), as a result of which the romantic ideal of the man as a "white knight" coming to the woman's "rescue" became increasingly obsolete. A white knight husband too quickly becomes a feudal lord, who, for the economically self-sufficient woman, is much less appealing than an equal partner. The next step was the separation of sexuality from reproduction (thanks to the widespread availability of contraception and artificial insemination), leading to the present-day "plastic sexuality."[43] The goal of this whole process is the liberation and emancipation of intimate relations from all sorts of external factors. This isn't limited to economic or reproductive issues. The ultimately desired form is precisely that of the "pure relationship," that is, one in which nothing is assumed *a priori* (or taken for granted by virtue of indisputable custom) and in which everything (the division of roles, how time is spent) is subject to constant negotiation. This, of course, is simply a bearing toward which, Giddens claims, our "being together" is heading today. Moreover, the crucial element of this new model is autonomy, which Giddens understands to be "the capacity of individuals to be self-reflective and self-determining."[44] In the end, being together serves no other purpose than the "successful realisation of the reflexive project of self" by each partner. Romantic love, as discussed above, is inherently contradictory as well, but in a different way. On the one hand, it approaches the fierce passion, what is referred to as *amour passion*, and on the other it is supposed to find fulfillment in marriage, a permanent relationship in which passion inevitably dies out, or at best gives way to kindness, attachment, etc. As we know, men and women found different ways of coping with this difficulty. The former imposed and reinforced double moral standards by seeking passion in the arms of mistresses and prostitutes,[45] only retiring to the family home for respite after their adventures in "the world." Women faced more difficult circumstances, but, according to Giddens, it was they who extracted from romantic love what had always been most important: its connection to self-realization. Prior to the sexual and economic emancipation of women, this self-realization was only superficial; it existed more as a germ of an idea. A married woman was dependent on her husband; in keeping with the bourgeois notion of marriage, she became his property. At the same time, according to a logic somewhat resembling Hegel's lordship and bondage, it was she, and not her lord/husband (who found "realization" in other pursuits such as work and extramarital romantic conquests) who elevated their intimate relationship to a higher level. It was she who demanded emotional commitment, attention, etc., all the while remaining in the subservient role of the house slave. Once women largely abandoned their subordinate status, or, more precisely, fought for and achieved a higher status, the doors to love in the sense of a pure relationship stood wide open before them. But what was the structural contradiction of the latter? Giddens finds it in the paradox of commitment:

> To generate commitment and develop a shared history, an individual must give of herself to the other. That is, she must

provide, in word and deed, some kind of guarantees to the other that the relationship can be sustained for an indefinite period. Yet a present-day relationship is not, as marriage once was, a "natural condition" whose durability can be taken for granted short of certain extreme circumstances. It is a feature of the pure relationship that it can be terminated, more or less at will, by either partner at any particular point.[46]

Giddens' vision contains a certain weakness, namely the assumption that the tendency of compulsion (neurotic love as mutual dependence) to wane in relationships, and of autonomy and mutual respect of boundaries (a feature of friendship) to grow plots some general and irreversible trend in contemporary Western societies. As is often the case, things are not quite as clear cut. In quantitative or statistical terms, these changes probably affect a small portion of the population (educated urban dwellers with cultural and economic capital at their disposal). The extent to which these changes foretell a more global transformation is a question that remains to be answered. Without treading into the realm of futurology, it is worth noting that the anxiety that produces compulsion is not a result of any mistake. As the psychoanalytic revisionists mentioned earlier pointed out, its very real foundations lie in the dominant social relations. For this reason, the notion of the modern-day couple as a pair of people who remain together until their relationship is terminated, whenever they please, who are not dependent on their relationship and treat it solely as part of their self-creation, isolated from material needs and considerations, and, finally, who are self-reliant and free of any anxiety, seems to be founded on a certain illusion. In this illusion, self-determination and total agency appear to exist under conditions conducive to precisely the opposite: mounting isolation, alienation, exclusion, and extreme economic instability. The roots of Giddens' lack of economic and psychological realism may lie in his political stance, in his delusions about the "Third Way," which, as it is now clear, failed to offer a serious alternative to neoliberal rule. This, however, is a separate matter. What relevance do these difficulties have to our discussion of friendship? Thus far we have primarily discussed how intimate relationships, shaped in the modern era by the ideal of romantic love, could rid themselves at least partially of their compulsive, neurotic character by strengthening the element of friendship, thus granting the individuals more space, in a sense, and enabling the further proliferation of other types of friendships. The question is: how do we strengthen that element when neurosis is still a mass phenomenon, and anxiety is deeply anchored in the structure of the modern subject? The simplest answer would be that we must begin by changing the circumstances, that is, the social conditions in which the institutions of marriage and the family reproduce. However, in doing so, we would avoid one illusion (everyone is or can be a self-contained, autonomous subject whose relations with others are based on freedom and equality) while immediately stumbling into another. It's hard to believe today the old saw that once the "objective" issues (particularly economic ones) have been taken care of by "the revolution," all of the "subjective" (moral, psychological) ones will be resolved automatically. And it's equally hard to believe in the opposite sequence of events: a spiritual or mental revolution that would just as automatically entail the creation of a more egalitarian society. In fact, both of these issues ("objective" and "subjective") are equally objective in nature, intersecting, again, in a real and concrete nexus. It is the nexus in which we live, think, act, and feel, taking part in its slow transformations, while also influencing it, to a certain extent, with our own practices.

The "transformation of intimacy" toward relationships that are less compulsive, freer, and based on autonomy requires actual dedication and real effort on the part of the men and women living together in various and increasingly "patchwork-like" configurations that, up until recently, would have been unimaginable within the confines of bourgeois morality. But intimacy isn't everything. What role could friendship play in affecting the forces and processes leading to broader social change? To ask this question correctly, we must step outside the traditional understanding of friendship as a bond shared by individuals. The expansion of the model of the closed family (that is, one based on compulsion) doesn't just diminish the rightfully important role of individual friendships beyond the jurisdiction of the family, so to speak; it also weakens, in the most general sense, our bonds with the people with whom we have to "get along" in society. The fact that the latter does not strike us as a community of friends has other causes, as well.

Chapter 3

The Pathos of Closeness

But there is another kind of love, where the union is from the instincts of nature and the laws of consanguinity, whereby those of the same tribe, wives and parents, and brothers and children are naturally preferred to others, a thing which we find is the case not only with mankind but with all birds and beasts.
John Cassian, The Conferences of the Desert Fathers (XVI)

To speak about friendship in a supra-individual context, to think of it as a bond shared by all of society, much less a global community of people, seems to be a confusion of terms or naïveté. One of the things that sets modern society apart from its pre-modern precursors is that its cohesion is guaranteed by regulations of a formal, particularly legal, nature. Friendship, on the other hand, is something we think of in terms of a private affect, one that is unassociated with institutions, rules, etc. In this sense, such a broad understanding of friendship would be a confusion of terms or levels. From the psychological standpoint, meanwhile, it would be naïve to envision a large group whose members were bound by true friendship, considering how difficult it is to maintain friendships at a much smaller scale. Moreover, as history teaches us, such naïveté—or, rather, this naïve language used to describe social or geopolitical relations— frequently serves as ideological cover for all sorts of machinations of power. We all know the truth behind the "fraternal friendship of the peoples" in the Eastern Block, for example. All of these objections are valid as long as we begin with a psychological understanding of friendship and subsequently attempt to apply that same meaning of the term to social or political phenomena. A cursory glance at the history of friendship as a philosophical concept, however, reveals that this narrow psychological meaning is only one of many. The categorical problem here is one of a different nature, namely, how to express the psychology of friendship as the concretization of a more abstract logic. But before we address this issue, we must first examine other levels, other concretizations of this logic of friendship. In particular, what is its political meaning? How can we employ this word in a collective context without veering into utopian thinking or using it in a purely metaphorical sense?

According to a saying traditionally ascribed to Aristotle, "He who has friends can have no true friend." This is the wording cited by Diogenes Laertius,[1] and a similar observation is found in the few passages Aristotle devotes to friendship in the *Nicomachean Ethics*.[2] They seem to harmonize with the philosopher's sense of reason, his pursuit of measure in all things. Summarizing his argument about the optimal number of friends, Aristotle states in the ninth book: "The number of one's friends must be limited, and should perhaps be the largest number with whom one can constantly associate."[3] Aristotle's authority testifies that friendship is only possible at a small scale, and that it is a mistake to be excessive in one's friendship (in other words, to attempt to encompass too many people with it). Something certainly connects us to those numerous others, but it is not friendship. The latter cannot, therefore, have a political meaning or refer to relations between people within the broader community of the *polis*. Contemporary authors, indulging their philological inquisitiveness, have discovered, however, that the original version of the saying cited above was not *oi philos, oudeis philos* (which one might translate as R.D. Hicks did in the English edition of the *Lives of Eminent Philosophers*), but: *o philoi, oudeis philos*. This form of the phrase, prior to its modification and clarification in the early seventeenth century by the Genevan philologist Isaac Casaubon,[4] is much more puzzling. The fact remains, of course, that in the *Ethics* Aristotle utters the aforementioned statement about the appropriate measure of friendship. But what are we to make of his cryptic words? Rendered in English, the phrase would read simply: "O, my friends, there is no friend." It appears to contain a paradox: a simultaneous affirmation and negation of friendship, perhaps even the very possibility thereof. But why not venture a different, less obvious interpretation? Can it be ruled out that Aristotle was implying something contrary to the teachings laid in his own writings: that *only* friends (*philoi*) exist, but a friend (*philos*), in the singular, does not? Not without reason, Derrida adopted this enigmatic phrase not merely as his motto, but as a refrain that would resurface in various forms throughout his lectures about friendship, provoking ever new interpretations. We will return to the book that resulted from these interpretative efforts,[5] as it directly addresses the possibility/impossibility of the politics of friendship. Continuing for a moment our discussion of Aristotle, it is worth mentioning that despite this clearly defined boundary or limit, and despite this conviction that it is not good to maintain friendships with too many people, the philosopher also discusses, elsewhere, friendship in the political context. In fact, this perspective has an extensive tradition, and its legitimacy is based on a principle, cited earlier, which by Plato and Aristotle's time had become an old adage: *koina ta ton philon*. "All things are common among friends," not just meaning material goods, the literal sense of the word "things." Friendship creates a human community that surpasses the personal relations shared by individuals. It was for this reason that it played such an important role in the Pythagorean community.[6] And it was because of this that Aristotle associated friendship with justice: "The objects and the personal relationships with which friendship is concerned appear... to be the same as those which are the sphere of justice. For in every partnership we find mutual rights of some sort, and also friendly feeling."[7] He goes on to distinguish between three forms of friendship corresponding to the three basic types of political communities, which he calls constitutions: kingship, aristocracy, and timocracy. Interestingly, he superimposes a familial code onto the subject of his analysis. And so the *philia* between a monarch and his subjects, a relationship involving "beneficence" and "doing good," corresponds to "the friendship of a father for his child"; the relation on which the aristocratic system is based resembles that between a husband and his wife, in which "the better party receives the larger share of good"; finally, in the constitution that Aristotle calls timocracy, in which "all citizens shall be equal and shall be good," "friendship between brothers" flourishes.[8] There is a significant fact worth noting here: it is perhaps not entirely irrelevant that the modern world, born of the pangs of revolution, bore on its banners not just the slogans of liberty and equality, but also fraternity. Is there some particular association between fraternity, friendship, and egalitarian-libertarian—that is, broadly democratic—politics? Aristotle, as we know, considered timocracy the least perfect of the three constitutions; he held democracy in even lower regard, seeing it as a perverted or degenerate form of timocracy. Nevertheless, of all the forms of government studied by the ancient philosopher, only democracy is the subject of active deliberation today, and remains a fundamental unsolved political problem. The debate on its proper meaning, the "distortions" of democratic ideas, the lack or deficit of "true" democracy, etc., has not died down, but has instead become increasingly intense. If this association in fact exists, then the question about true democracy cannot be divorced from the question about the meaning of fraternity and friendship, and the causes of the distortions that continue to plague these two ideas, as well.

It is this nexus, among others, that Jacques Derrida explores in his highly interesting book *The Politics of Friendship*. Its general approach is, of course, that of deconstruction. The particular urgency of this deconstruction is particularly evident in the case of fraternity, which, after all, establishes a certain particular as a universal. Citizens who fight for liberty and equality, and against tyranny, are brothers; this raises the question: What about the sisters? The tragic fate of Olympia de Gouges shows that brothers were not keen to share with them their hard-won liberties. However, the significance of what Derrida calls "phratrocentrism" lies deeper still. Even if they were to welcome women into their fraternal community, thus in a sense recognizing sisters as capable of being brothers, this act would be marked by asymmetry. What must a sister do to be worthy of the title of brother? What attributes must she acquire, and which ones must she rid herself of? Fraternity that does not distinguish between brothers and sisters, or, as Derrida puts it in his analysis of the writings of Jules Michelet, a "fraternity beyond fraternity," a greater or truer form of fraternity, essentially condemns us to a situation in which "one never renounces that which one claims to renounce, and which returns in myriad ways, through symptoms and disavowals."[9] Similarly, the universalization of the phallus or the Name of the Father will never enable psychoanalysis to "disavow" phallocentrism. As for the philosophical concept of friendship in its various versions and transformations throughout history, it reveals, upon closer examination, an even more powerful charge of ambivalence. Derrida spends several hundred pages describing it with his typical passion for detail, but it would seem that its roots lie in the ancient beginnings of philosophical reflections on *philia*, specifically, the ties between friendship and that which we see as our own, familiar, similar, or native. Many historians point out that in the Homeric Age, the word *philos* was used as an adjective to describe something close, not just in the sense that another person can be close or dear to us, but also—even especially—in the sense of "closeness" that defines the members of our own bodies. "Since 'dear' seems inappropriate in these connections, some scholars have taken *philos* as equivalent to a possessive adjective, 'one's own,' and have drawn the further conclusion that this is the primary or original significance of the word."[10] From the historical and philological point of view, this matter remains a subject of debate; there are scholars who question this line of reasoning, but even if we were to agree that the adjective *philos* means something more than just a certain type of property, and that it refers to an affect, an inclination toward another person, there remains the question: to whom is this affect primarily directed? What does it mean, for example, that nearly all ancient authors who wrote about friendship were using a familial code? Fraternity, after all, leaves out not just sisters, but all those who do not belong to the family. In ancient Greece, *philia*, in its basic sense, was a bond between members of the family, the clan, the *genos*. Even the broader community of friends, one spanning all of the Hellenes, for example, was a homogeneous one, and, as Derrida writes, that friendship was "homophilial" in nature."[11] Furthermore, the emphasis on internal homogeneity becomes greater the more obviously this homogeneous community is founded on a certain fantasy or fiction, as has often been pointed out in reference to the modern idea of the nation. It is this constitutive fabrication that must be defended by subjecting it to radical naturalization. There is no other purpose to political discourses that "[appeal] to birth, to nature or to the nation—indeed, to nations or to the universal nation of human brotherhood."[12] The philosophical reflection on friendship belongs to this pathos of closeness and kinship. Or at least this is true insofar as it references its own mythical, archaic origins. Is there anything more Greek than *The Odyssey*? And is it not the fullest manifestation of this inability to step beyond the boundary circumscribing what is "one's own" and familiar? Many contemporary thinkers, among them Levinas, have made this observation. The book that established our culture's paradigmatic understanding of the journey or voyage depicts it as a return to the point of departure, as a homecoming.[13] Odysseus cries out in the palace of Alcinous: "But as for myself, grant me a rapid convoy home / from all my loved ones [*philon apo*]—how long I have suffered!"[14] The gods heed his pleas, but what's most important is that his friends are waiting at home; therefore, as long as the hero is traveling, he remains far from them. The notion that he could make true friends in a faraway land, among strangers, was incompatible with the Homeric spirit. In the philosophy of friendship, this finds its reflection in the recurring motif of *similarity* as a principle by which people choose friends and the basis of the bond between them. To be sure, in Plato's *Lysis*—which has many features of early Socratic dialog, leading to aporia rather than to a positive conclusion—the matter remains unsettled: the interlocutors are unable to determine whether friends are bound together by their similarity[15] or whether, in this case, opposites attract.[16] Little is achieved by replacing the category of "like" with that of "belonging."[17] Finally, Socrates gives up and says: "If neither the loved nor the loving, nor the like nor the unlike, nor the good nor the belonging, nor all the rest that we have tried in turn—they are so many that I, for one, fail to remember any more—well, if none of these is a friend, I am at a loss for anything further to say."[18] A different view can be found in the *Republic*, where Plato stresses that citizens are to be "akin and friendly."[19] Aristotle, meanwhile, states authoritatively that all friendship is "prompted by similarity of some sort."[20] In his view, "amity consists in equality and similarity, especially the similarity of those who are alike in virtue."[21]

Which depiction of friendship is more suitable: the more contemporary one, which emphasizes proximity, or the earlier one, in which *philia* applies only to that which is close, "one's own," and familiar? Perhaps this question shouldn't even be posed in terms of suitability. Perhaps there exist different kinds and different "politics" of friendship. That is precisely why Derrida—who constantly unmasks the entanglement between the traditional discourse on friendship and our deep-seated tendency toward homogenization, the practical and political dimensions of which have often had terrible consequences—simultaneously attempts to outline a discourse of another type. Unlike the former established and dominant discourse, one legitimated by its proper and ancient provenance, this alternative discourse of friendship is merely possible and is expressed in the Nietzschean "perhaps," which Derrida treats as a messianic promise of sorts.

> Would it still make sense to speak of democracy when it would no longer be a question (no longer in question as to what is essential or constitutive) of a country, nation, even of state or citizen—in other words, *if at least one still keeps to the accepted use of this word,* when it would no longer be a political question?[22]

Derrida calls this other democracy—a result of the deconstruction of the very genealogical principle—"hyperdemocracy," granting it the status of something "to come" (à *venir*). What is to come is in no way preordained. This is not Fukuyama's "liberal democracy," which just needs to overcome a few technical hurdles before it achieves ultimate victory, or is already victorious, unbeknownst to some. To Derrida, the democracy to come is synonymous with justice[23] and is necessary only in the sense of something indispensable, something we must have if we hope not to be doomed to that which is *called* democracy and, more generally, politics.

The latter, Carl Schmitt cautions us, is based on the fundamental distinction of friend and enemy. "The political enemy need not be morally evil or aesthetically ugly; he need not appear as an economic competitor," he writes. "He is, nevertheless, the other, the stranger; and it is sufficient for his nature that he is…existentially something different and alien."[24] It is telling that Schmitt devotes so much space to defining the political enemy, clarifying the distinction between the *hostis* and the *inimicus*, while overlooking the other element— the very first one he mentioned, in fact. What matters here is the enemy, because enmity (culminating in war) constitutes the essence of politics: it is possible to ennoble this enmity by emphasizing its connection to the Greek *polemos*, etc., but it remains a fact that from this perspective, enmity is primal. What would a community be if it were not based on the exclusion of the stranger, the other? An entirely nonpolitical union, at most. Furthermore, to be constituted as a political entity, it must recognize the stranger to be an enemy who threatens its values or even its very existence. In this sense, even if one cannot *de facto* have political enemies without having friends, and vice versa, *de iure* there is no symmetry between Schmitt's categories. Friends, "one's own" people, are friends in the political only insofar as they face some enemy, insofar as they are allies in some conflict or war. Lacking that, they would be situated entirely beyond the polemic principle. Enemies without friends, or belligerents in a *bellum omnium contra omnes*, are also nonpolitical, or not yet political, but remain at least in a state of war. War is the *arche*, the source and ever-present foundation of the political, and therefore a society of friends without enemies or eternal peace cannot be its *telos*; rather, it signifies the negation thereof. In a world defined by this political theory and practice, the absence of an enemy looming on the horizon is highly alarming. Derrida was perfectly aware of this in his contemplation of friendship, in the early 1990s.

> From the "fall-of-the-Berlin-Wall," or from the "end-of-communism," the "parliamentary-democracies-of-the-capitalist-Western-world" would find themselves without a principle enemy. The effects of this destructuration would be countless: the "subject" in question would be looking for new reconstitutive enmities; it would multiply "little wars" between nation states; it would seek to pose itself, to find

repose, through opposing still identifiable adversaries—China, Islam?[25]

All of the above are conditional statements; Derrida's aim is precisely to challenge that logic, to find a breach in its walls. And yet that is exactly what happened. The end of a bi-polar world divided by the Iron Curtain coincided with the proclamation of a "clash of civilizations," and Islamic terrorism soon replaced communism as the "principle enemy" of the West.

For Derrida, the entanglement between the philosophical discourse on friendship and "ethnocentrism" (thinking in terms of what is "our own") is inevitable, just as it is inevitable for thinking to be entangled in metaphysics. For this reason, the hyperdemocracy-to-come, which corresponds to the messianic order, is merely alluded to, following his analysis of all the undecidables and paradoxes, as a certain impossible possibility. Radical hope is, in a way, the complement of the caution that characterizes deconstruction. However, would it not be possible, at least tentatively, to reverse this pattern and propose—rather recklessly, or at least much more explicitly—a different understanding of friendship, one that would not make of it something not-of-this-world? Such an attempt should necessarily entail a radical departure from Schmitt and his understanding of politics, replacing it with a completely different, in a sense opposite, understanding. The place of the transcendental principle of enmity, which precedes even the distinction between friend and enemy, and from which the latter two follow as the basis of war or conflict, must be taken by a greater principle of friendship. It should also serve as the transcendental base for political alliances as well as conflicts. Without the latter, a society of friends would at best be a fiction, and at worst a space in which all conflict is artificially suppressed in the name of undisturbed harmony. Theorists of the political have correctly pointed to the positive and emancipatory function of the *polemos*. At the same time, overcoming the primacy of war in the field of political theory has proved extraordinarily difficult. The language of politics is the language of enmity. Consequently, it is best to think of friendship as a *social* principle, and to only later connect it to political conflict.

Philosophy and the social sciences provide a surprising number of theoretical tools with which to perform this *volte-face*. More than a century ago, the Polish anarchist thinker and activist Edward Abramowski wrote in the cooperative magazine *Społem*: "That which is destroyed by capitalism and slavery, namely prosperity and the nobility of life, is salvaged and rebuilt by cooperativism, by the cooperation of human friendships; it not only creates new social conditions, but strives to create a new type of human, one that is free and strong because he is part of a pack, and because he understands and feels friendship."[26] Friendship as a transcendental social principle is just that: the principle of cooperation or action for the common good, contrasted with the principle of competition and personal gain. This concept of friendship has been studied by numerous theorists, many of whom work outside the narrowly defined boundaries of political philosophy. In the aftermath of the last capitalist crisis, it is becoming increasingly clear that humanity must either abandon the rapacious exploitation of resources and learn to cooperate with each other, other species, and the rest of nature, or it will unleash a social, political, or natural disaster of unprecedented scale. Any truly emancipatory social movement must therefore be based, at some level and to some extent, on this understanding of the principle of friendship. This is even true of those movements that—like the anarchist movement— have traditionally been deeply suspicious to the collective, to being part of a "pack," as Abramowski calls it. The evolution of anarchism—which passed through a phase of nihilistic, or at least radically individualistic, rejection of any personal obligations to the collective, and has since become one of the pillars of the resurgence of cooperativism—is extraordinarily informative in this context. At its core, the challenge we face is figuring out how to combat the culture of selfishness and personal gain at all cost, without falling into a herd mentality; how to reclaim the idea of the collective without descending into collectivism. In this sense, present-day anarchists are testing solutions for a possible future.

Where does the axis of political conflict lie within this realm of cooperation-as-friendship? There is no doubt that conflict is necessary, that a reversal of the dominant trend—one that has rapidly accelerated, propelled by neoliberal reforms and the dismantling of the welfare state—requires the political mobilization of anger, resistance, perhaps even enmity among the proverbial 99 percent of the global population. To be sure, the character of this trend is civilizational rather than political, and cannot be reduced to the victory of particular parties or factions. Therefore, its reversal will likely be neither quick nor the exclusive result of political action. Demographics, processes associated with climate change, economic crises—all of these factors (which now threaten to cause a disaster or series of connected disasters) may play a much more decisive role. This is not to say that we should wait for a global catastrophe in hopes that a new order will emerge from its wake. The lines of division between the forces whose actions follow the logic of the common good, and those who are ruining the planet and exploiting human life as a means of amassing capital are already clearly defined, at least *a priori* (their precise location in each individual case is a matter of tactical analysis). The topography of the battlefield is constantly shifting; new subjects and partial stakes continue to emerge, but the fundamental conflict in a sense remains the same. This is precisely the conflict Abramowski and other classics of socialism/anarchism wrote about: the selfish culture of profit and domination versus a culture of equality and cooperation. It is clear that the transcendental principle of friendship does not necessitate the adoption of a discourse of harmony and unity that would mask the conflict. On the contrary: it must be rejected in the name of that very principle, one that at most sets a distant horizon for today's battles. Returning to Schmitt and his theory of politics, the true enemy, from his point of view, was not so much communism or even Bolshevism (that other or stranger looming at the gates of Western civilization) as it was liberalism, an internal enemy whose extreme duplicity involved denying the very principle of war, blurring the lines of the existential conflict ("It's either us or them") in parliamentary twaddle. We could similarly say that the true enemies of the politics of friendship are those who adhere to the principle of enmity as a universal, irreducible law. Stating it in such terms naturally raises a number of doubts and brings to mind disconcerting associations. Would a "society of friends" that combats and excludes enemies of friendship not result, sooner or later, in terror?[27] And, on the other hand, isn't the politics of friendship too broad a term, bordering on the commonplace—not unlike juxtaposition of the principle of profit and exploitation with that of cooperation? We are, after all, living in the twenty-first century, and have become aware of the ambiguity and complexity of our situation, in which the myriad political battlefields of our time cannot by reduced to a common denominator. There are many movements today fighting for a "better world," but it won't come any closer to becoming a reality, nor will there emerge any shared understanding of that world or the path that leads to it.

Stepping down momentarily from this (perhaps excessively) high level of generalization: how could these deliberations on the principle of friendship and its connection to politics be applied to the specific circumstances we now find ourselves in as a result of the so-called migrant crisis? This crisis, as it is often said, involves the migrants themselves (their number and their potential for "extremist" behavior) as well as the model of common living in their destination countries. Those who stress that the current multicultural model has been exhausted, and was perhaps badly constructed from the beginning, are also correct. People who respond to the migrants with xenophobia and aggression (even in places where these migrants have not yet arrived, and perhaps have no intention of settling) therefore draw the conclusion that the current situation demands a return to closed, homogeneous communities that guard their borders from strangers. Only by doing so, the argument goes, will we protect ourselves from a far more serious crisis that is the "Islamization of Europe," a "wave of terrorism," or—in the mildest version of the claim—the creation of ghettos inhabited by immigrants who "refuse to integrate" into the culture of broader society. While it is difficult to debate the first two narratives, as they are too deeply seated in prejudice and irrational fear, the matter of integration touches upon a significant issue. It is, after all, a question of social cohesion, of the bond that cements people who live in a particular society—and not just those who arrive from abroad, fleeing war, hunger, etc. Every individual integrates with society through the process of socialization. The question is, what pattern does this process follow, and does this model hold up when applied to an influx of people previously socialized in different circumstances? The belief that we ought to strive for peaceful coexistence between people of different cultures, each of whom will nurture their own uniqueness and differences, presupposes what can be described as identity thinking, and applies it equally to the members of the "native" culture in a particular area. Let native Frenchmen cultivate their Frenchness alongside North African migrants, who in turn have the right to do the same, as long as they submit to the rule of law and, crucially, contribute to the production process. To each his own identity, with the common denominator being the law and the market...Yet as soon as the market can no longer absorb the influx of labor power, which not only refuses to "go home," but begins to challenge certain core principles (such as the French doctrine of *laïcité*), a dangerous internal conflict starts to brew.

Naturally, no philosophy of friendship could provide solutions to these complex problems, but it can be useful in one regard: it can point to the possibility of an alternative means of integration.

But isn't recognizing distinct identities not the very meaning of friendship, at least when the coexistence of people in a society is concerned? Not necessarily. In our previous discussion of intimate relations, we mentioned the matter of respecting another person's *autonomy* as a fundamental principle of friendship (in contrast to possessive, objectifying neurotic love). Although the idea of autonomy is sometimes associated in philosophy with the concept of identity, it can also be understood in opposition to this concept and its attendant practices. In that case, autonomy primarily means the capacity of the individual to distance themselves from any attributes, including ones that constitute their identity. Friendship means respecting another's autonomy, not their identity; it grants them the right to be someone other than who they are, and it invariably sees in them something more than can be reduced to their being "a Muslim," "a conservative," "a woman," etc.[28] Scholars who have discoursed on the subject of friendship have rarely devoted much space to the moment in which it fades or even turns into its own opposite.[29] Yet this moment is a significant one. We often say of a former friend (or one who is growing distant): "After all, she's just a...", "She's nothing more than a...", "She's really nothing but a...". Such an encapsulation of the other in one identity or another is a contradiction of friendship, which always leaves the other some leeway, the option of surpassing every defined form. A society that functions in this manner is one into which a foreigner can integrate with relative ease. Someone might rightly observe that this kind of society is itself based on exclusion: it excludes those who perceive themselves and others as having a "strong" identity. Or that what this boils down to is an eradication of all differences, as in the concept of the melting pot, where they are blended together into a mixture with no defining characteristics.

In the case of the former, namely, the paradox of a weak identity that is founded on the negation and exclusion of a strong identity, it is hard to find any decisive arguments. It seems that the fundamental fault line actually runs not between "civilizations" (Western civilization and the Muslim world), but between these two approaches to the question of identity (along with their corresponding sets of practices).[30] Indeed, if we were to compare the jihadists fighting under the banner of the Islamic State to Anders Breivik and other self-styled guardians of Christian Europe, we would discover that they have plenty in common. To quote, once again, Houellebecq's last novel: "For these Muslims, the real enemy—the thing they fear and hate—isn't Catholicism. It's secularism. It's laicism. It's atheist materialism."[31] Theweleit adds that: "Breivik is envious of the Muslim man's unquestionable power position (just like the Nazis, who were principally envious of the 'Jews' and wanted to be the 'chosen people' themselves. By exterminating the Jewish people, they hoped to magically assume their power.) In structural terms, Breivik *is* a patriarchal Muslim, as well as Norse-Christian anti-Semite, and cultist Germanic SS-Mann."[32] What is relevant here, however, isn't just a given society's attitude toward women or its propensity toward violence. What is being guarded, in both instances, is an insular cultural community that imposes on the individual particular models of acting, thinking, and feeling. It is to be a homogeneous community where everyone "knows their place" and in which roles (especially gender roles) are predetermined. It should come as no surprise, therefore, that while each side claims to dislike or even hate the other (Islamophobia on one side, philippics against "crusaders" on the others), their true and common enemy is what Breivik calls "cultural Marxism" and what jihadists claim is the "corruption" of Western society. In their minds, these terms most likely stand in for a number of interconnected things (which aren't necessarily associated, at least not in this way), but we can probably venture the claim that if they in fact refer to something real, then that something is the "loosening" of traditional cultural norms that defines late modernity, the blurring of the traditional division of roles, and the myriad trajectories and models among which the individual may choose during the process of socialization.

If this is true, then are those who portray the current conflict as a clash between "fundamentalism" and "liberal democracy" correct? Yes and no. Yes, insofar as both liberalism and democracy are premised on exerting less community pressure than traditional societies, and respect human autonomy in the sense discussed above. No, if by liberal democracy we mean the form into which it is collapsing before our very eyes, namely, a system in which the power wielded by the people is increasingly illusory, in which people have the right to choose but lack any real choice, and in which the range of choice is restricted to a minimum by the power of capital, unleashed by unbridled economic neoliberalism. This system (and the rightful disappointment and indignation it provokes) is more likely the reason why fundamentalist tendencies are growing in strength today. Consequently — to refer once more to the idea of the melting pot — it is increasingly urgent that we find a different common denominator or an alternative means of "mixing" cultures. If the American melting pot also appears to be overheating, it is because the common denominator — that is, the rules of the free market — do not contribute to the establishment of the common, but are instead exacerbating divisions, widening the gap between the rich and the poor, and with it the gap separating races and ethnic communities. Perhaps the time has come to abandon the American dream of rising from rags to riches, and replace it with a new dream of friendship as the fundamental social bond.

A different politics and, more broadly, a different practice of friendship is possible, though very difficult under present circumstances. The realm of intimate relations is plagued by the mass phenomenon of neurosis, which poisons not just love in its modern-day form, but relations between friends, as well. The latter seem appropriate only within biographically-determined limits (childhood, adolescence), or serve a compensatory function, granting respite from the disappointing vicissitudes of romantic and married life. In the worst case, they take the form of men's associations based on hierarchy and violence. There is gradually increasing public awareness of the fact that friendships, at least in Western culture, are too rare and too weak. More and more is being said about the consequences of this, described in the current jargon as "heightened stress," the fundamental cause of which isn't just work, but also family and home issues. The philosophers of old would simply have observed that no one can be happy without friends with whom to share their lives. In the social and political domains, as well, friendship is a far-from-essential type of bond. On the one hand, the capitalist (neoliberal) principle of competition has placed the individual, the entrepreneur of the self, in a state of constant mobilization, competing with others for various kinds of capital, of which economic capital is the most important, but not only, form. On the other hand, and in a sense in response to the resultant withering away of the community, there are increasingly visible tendencies toward separatism, xenophobia, and the desire to live in insular communities among "one's own," cemented by a fear of, and hostility toward, strangers. Friendship is thereby marginalized either by the logic of selfish interests (or exploited in their pursuit), or takes on an ominous, ethnocentric form that turns slogans about the clash of civilizations into a self-fulfilling prophecy. But there's more. Of all the meanings the philosophical tradition has ascribed to friendship, the one perhaps least comprehensible to us is that which saw it as a principle cementing the entire universe: not just relations between private individuals or a bond shared by the citizens of the *polis*, but something that makes the world function as a harmonious whole. This is certainly caused in part by our modern habit of thinking in terms of the psychological and political rather than the metaphysical, our suspicion of the very concept of the whole, of the speculations about universal principles, etc. It's hard to deny these processes and ignore their impact on contemporary philosophy. Yet there's another factor at play here. We live in an era of neurosis and competition, but also one marked by the unprecedented destruction of living conditions on our planet. For this reason, the Pythagorean notion of the universal *philia* as the principle governing the universe seems distant, even exotic. When humans talk about the universe, it is naturally a human universe, which in turn means one that is not only shaped by particular categories of thought, but also marked by the way in which humans inhabit it. But our present way of being in the world can hardly be described as "inhabiting"; it resembles rather the behavior of a person who, having broken into someone's house, ransacks it, ruins it, and then…well, the analogy ends there, because short of fantasies about colonizing outer space, we have nowhere to run with our loot. If the Earth was once a welcoming place for humans, it was only insofar as humans extended the same kindness in return, as required by the principle of reciprocity.[33] Problems of this sort, once contemplated by Heidegger, in his later years, and by some thinkers associated with the Frankfurt School, are nowadays more likely to be seen as a kind of philosophical folklore that is the domain of rabid environmentalists rather than a subject of professional reflection. And yet, at the most fundamental level, these rabid environmentalists are correct: the position humans have assumed vis-à-vis the rest of nature is simply untenable if we hope to prevent the grimmest catastrophic scenarios. Even now, as the probability of the catastrophe grows, life is becoming increasingly devoid of all the benefits of amicable coexistence with the world. We prefer to push these facts out of our minds, telling ourselves that "it's not that bad" or that technology will still "save us," that scientists are surely hard at work on solutions to all our problems, and that we just need to discover a groundbreaking method of harnessing renewable energy, etc. In the end, all of this might prove to be wishful thinking. That's why, aside from deneuroticizing our personal relations, basing our social relations on cooperation, and abandoning strong identity projects, it is urgent that we fundamentally transform our being in the world. And while this certainly requires us to change our "attitude" or "way of thinking," it is still strictly tied to other less abstract issues, not the least of which is politics, which has become more than just biopolitics, but also—quite directly—ecopolitics. It's "capitalism vs. the climate," as Naomi Klein summarizes it in the subtitle of her 2014 book.[34] But it's more than that, if we accept the existence of an association between neurosis and the possessiveness that has defined our attitude toward the world.

What is perhaps needed, as Heidegger argued, is some *Gelassenheit*, a stance of "letting things be" in the world around us, abandoning the project and practice of subjugating not just other people, but also nonhuman reality; the expansion of the principle of friendship to all feeling beings and, further, onto the entire universe. However, if this is to be a global phenomenon, rather than one limited to various environmental niches, it cannot take place without radical changes in the political and economic status quo. Is this not another paradox of the positive politics of friendship? A powerful affective relation based on the respect of autonomy and distance, a collective that doesn't descend into collectivism, and now something along the lines of a quietist revolution, activism for the cause of withdrawal? Perhaps this series of paradoxes reflects some significant features or a deeper logic of friendship, at whatever level (psychological, social, cosmic) it is shared. Friendship is, above all else, about connections. It forms assemblages (comprising individuals, groups, species, etc.), establishes connections between elements, none of which occupy a dominant position. Otherwise, the logic of connections would be replaced with the logic of subsumption and belonging. The whole to which one belongs is defined by some dominant element, and for that reason even the idea of cosmic friendship connecting the elements of the universe should not appeal to the strong figure of the universe as a whole (in this sense differing from the traditional understanding). The universe of friendship is an infinity of connections, an infinite space in which beings mingle, but it is not synonymous with homogeneity—just as a society of friends mixes without blending, and an intimate relationship based on friendship connects individuals without melding them together and depriving them of their autonomy. Wholes and homogenizing tendencies are altogether real, but friendships are made in places where there occurs a weakening of the former; it is a kind of relation that is most easily entered when one abandons the order of belonging and inclusion, in a sense *betraying* it. The suspicion that friendship is a form of betrayal is not entirely unfounded, both at the level of intimate relations (as discussed above) and in social and political contexts (authorities often regard groups of friends with suspicion)—and even that of interspecies relations (the well-worn accusation of environmentalists and vegetarians "caring more about animals than they do about people"). Another characteristic of connections or assemblages of friendships is that they are productive, though not in the same sense as bonds based on belonging. Even in cases where, by their very nature, they create no "benefit" at the individual level, they still produce certain effects (Aristotle would say they strengthen virtue among friends). Even when—at the social level—they exceed the logic of survival, they are a condition for cooperation. This aspect is of particular significance today when it comes to the relation between humans and the world around them. The existing practice—or at least the modern one, Western in spirit—demands that we equate productivity with the harnessing of nature and the exploitation of its resources. Hence the not entirely unfounded fear that abandoning the project of controlling nature with technology will inevitably lead to a drastic decline in productivity, the loss of our civilizations' "achievements," a drop in living standards, and so on. We should approach this problem from a different perspective, however, and consider it in more abstract terms or using a broader understanding of production. We produce an unbelievable quantity of goods (products) that satisfy many different needs, but we also produce an enormous amount of other effects: from pollution to the sum of physical and mental suffering caused by living in a world geared toward this particular type of production and consumption. Leaving this model behind might limit the availability of all sorts of products from every corner of the globe, but it would have many positive consequences, as well. Productivity involves a highly complex balance.

This logic of connections and assemblages raises another important issue. Even if the spirit of friendship is currently in decline at all levels and in all areas, and even if the prospect of a politics based on the transcendental principle of friendship seems unlikely, if not impossible, it does not mean that we have no choice but to oscillate between visions of disaster and utopia. The disaster may yet occur, and it won't necessarily be a world-ending catastrophe: it is enough that the increasingly realistic prospect of Western countries descending into soft or hard fascism as they attempt to mitigate the perceived threat posed by the "Muslim world" comes to fruition. This outcome will not be prevented by conjuring up visions of utopian projects, but only by limited, local, and actual practices that pursue the better scenario right now, step by step, through trial and error. Utopian thinking, in the sense of attempts to imagine a perfect or even relatively decent world happening *all at once*, is at odds with what can be described as the elementary empiricism of the practices of friendship. Connections are made one after the other, and the elements that make up assemblages undergo constant reconfiguration; there is no final state to speak of, no ultimate configuration. Empiricism is about experimentation rather than all-encompassing projects. Even though neurosis is deeply rooted in our mental structures; even though we continue to over-invest, affectively and symbolically, in families and couples; even though we are tied to others by a relationship based on competition for dwindling resources or by an all-consuming community founded on hostility toward all things foreign; and even though our relationship to our planet is one of cruel, thoughtless exploitation—despite all of this, or perhaps precisely because of this, we must continue to experiment with new and different ways of living. We must do so in the name of loyalty—not to an Event that has already taken place or is yet to come, but to becoming-friendly of the world, which we can only hope to be a part of.

Afterword

I would like to conclude by examining a number of problematic issues that I skim over or omit entirely in this essay. The first matter, one that critical readers are certain to have noticed, is that the connection between the historical perspective adopted at the beginning of the text and the ethical-existential proposal presented later is not entirely clear. Our historical sense, if we apply it in the spirit of Nietzschean genealogy—as I have attempted to do—invariably reveals the richness and complexity of overlapping meanings that cannot be encapsulated in one unambiguous definition. Friendship is no exception. It has been understood and—perhaps more importantly—practiced in myriad, often contradictory ways. I write in Chapter One about the difficulties this raises for the researcher. Is there some common denominator to all the forms of friendship that have existed, continuously or intermittently, throughout history, aside from the word itself? Even the words (*philia, amicitia, amitié, friendship...*) change, for that matter, shifting from one semantic field to the next. However, when my focus shifts to the contemporary, that is, in the next two chapters, a particular understanding of friendship takes shape; some of its many historical meanings recede into the background, while others are emphasized and accentuated. Thus assembled from disparate elements, the concept provides a positive point of reference for a critique of the present, and perhaps even a foundation for a certain positive project. Are these two approaches not mutually exclusive in that they consider friendship from the perspective of historical nominalism, ridding it of all essence and precluding any substantive definition, and then proceed to project onto it some true sense that allows us to contrast friendship with other relations (romantic love, economic competition, belonging to a national community)? For now, I can only respond to this potential charge by emphasizing that the fundamental point of reference for my entire essay is the present; it is an analysis of the hermetic enclosure of contemporary life in the work-family-nation triangle. A history of the concept and practice of friendship has yet to be written; my goal, meanwhile, has been to envisage a form of common living that would evade the grasp of this triangle and the principles governing each of its constituent parts (neurotic compulsion, ruthless rivalry, and ingroup/outgroup logic). I concluded that friendship, as a concept, was well suited to this purpose, but not because it had some transhistorical essence; rather, it was because it embodied, in certain historical contexts, the meanings and qualities I wished to convey. These are precisely the meanings and qualities that I uncover and emphasize at the expense of the other, perhaps more numerous and dominant, ones, by addressing historical texts, including such classics as Aristotle and Kant. The manner in which I reference ancient authors is, in this sense, strategic— some might say exploitative—as I do not believe we should cultivate the myth of antiquity as some lost paradise to which we must return. The Greeks may be of use in our present predicament, but we should also keep in mind, for instance, that their lofty concept of friendship as a relation between men who encourage one another to persist in their virtue, above the realm of material concerns, was only possible because their material needs were provided for by the labor of their wives and slaves.

In the same vein, I contrast friendship not just with romantic love, but with work subordinate to the principle of competition and the insular national (or "cultural") community. Each of these three domains (the family, work, the nation) is based on some form of common-being, that is, community, even if we have come to think of modern work as something that must be complemented by some sort of community, due to the alienation that defines the economic sphere today. It would be easier to simply propose that we break out of this undoubtedly limiting, restrictive triangle by saying, "in Greek," that humans are truly free (or even truly human) only insofar as they are not forced to toil (*ponos*) and have a life outside of the family home (*oikos*). But that would be too easy, and perhaps even dangerous. After all fascists, as Theweleit convincingly argues, also attempted to liberate themselves from the monotony of family life (especially from their wives, with whom they were unable to establish a human relation) and the need to fight for survival in the bourgeois society of "merchants." They thus became warriors who fled their families into the hierarchical embrace of communities based on fraternity among soldiers. For this reason, I instead attempt to identify the principle governing each of the aforementioned realms and contrast it with the principle of friendship not as something that is necessarily extraneous to it, but as a principle that could work within their boundaries, either in opposition or in complement to those principles. Neither the nuclear family, nor capitalist labor relations, nor nations will last forever. But when they do finally disappear—assuming life on Earth doesn't disappear first—it will likely be more than a few generations from now. That is why, without engaging in utopian thinking, we must begin now to think about making life in existing communities more bearable in hopes that the factors instrumental to that bearability will one day become more widespread or even commonplace. It is precisely in this sense that I suggest we contrast/complement the neurotic desire to own and control, the compulsion and anxiety that underpins romantic love, the glue bonding the modern couple, with the principle of autonomy and the mutual respect of boundaries. What is left of love once the neurotic ingredient has been removed should be compatible with this understanding of friendship. I then juxtapose the principle of competition, which governs relations among people in the spheres of labor and production, with cooperation, which just as obviously is not and should not be external to labor (this is not to say, however, that it is only encountered at work).[1] The greatest challenge, in relative terms, was to consider friendship as an external/internal counterweight to the logic of national or cultural chauvinism. As Derrida demonstrates in his excellent, dense analyses, the matter is much more complicated than that, and throughout history the concept of friendship has almost always been marked by a characteristic predilection for the similar, the familiar, "one's own." Nevertheless, I make a modest attempt, in this context, to depict friendship not so much as the welcoming of "the other's otherness" — in the sense of a particular state, a paradoxical (anti)identity — but as becoming-the-other with others.

But shouldn't we undertake a more conceptual elaboration of this understanding of friendship, tentatively adopted for the purpose of confronting our present circumstances? Shouldn't we construct the concept of friendship departing from this strategic analysis? This was the aim of the section devoted to the abstract logic of friendship, with its rules of empiricism, connections, and productivity, but the results certainly leave much to be desired. Perhaps I should not have addressed this subject in the first place, knowing that I would go no further than a sketch, a preliminary outline. I leave this passage intact as a testimony to my incomplete attempt, with the knowledge that this is precisely one of the functions of the essay format: to facilitate attempts that do not always produce satisfactory results.

Although an abstract, conceptual study of the logic of friendship, in which analyses and descriptions of the present would provide a source of examples, rather than the very core of the discussion, as is the case in this essay, would simply require a separate text, it is hard to justify the theoretical shortcomings apparent in the passages devoted to a few particular issues. I refer specifically to the matter of desire and the fundamental ambiguity that appears in my discussion when I attempt to contrast friendship with romantic relations in the modern sense, that is, ones subject to the law of desiring the Other. While I conclude that neurosis does not, and need not, constitute the essence of desire *per se*, and that the sole and ultimate destiny of the latter is not predetermined by its neuroticization and oedipalization (along with the attendant compulsion and possessiveness), my characterization of friendship seems to overlook the matter of desire entirely. Does friendship still have anything to do with desire, or does it lead us outside its jurisdiction? Does an "outside" even exist? The question is relevant in that desire, thrown out through the front door, so to speak, it tends to come in through the back, reappearing in its most neurotic form. To posit that intimate relations should be based on friendship rather than romantic love may seem imprudent, and at best unrealistic. Intimate relationships, meaning ones involving a significant degree of closeness that is also a result of the erotic component, can never be completely purified of jealousy, for example. This feeling can be suppressed, but never completely. Isn't it better, as self-help book authors would argue, to try to "manage" it? Does friendship not owe at least part of its noble nature to the fact that it is (allegedly) above this tangle of problematic, extreme, and contradictory affects into which we are drawn by desire? To answer this question, we would have to create a new theory of desire or appeal to existing theories that show how desire can also assume a radically different form. I attempted to do just that, but only by alluding in the footnotes to the concept authored by Deleuze and Guattari. In the end, are we thinking of a different kind of desire, or something other than desire as such? I admittedly do not have a clear stance on this issue, and though my theoretical sympathies lie with the Deleuzian concept of desire, I am sometimes inclined toward this other "something." Perhaps it would be possible to imagine an affect ungoverned by the rules of *désir*. As horrifying as it might sound to modern minds reared on psychoanalysis, maybe, as Foucault argued, the "man of desire" is himself a product of particular historical (discursive and extradiscoursive) circumstances, which, like all circumstances, will one day disappear. In fact, not just psychoanalytic theory, but even the unconscious itself could turn out to be a product of a certain era, with its own expiration date, if you will. A person who experiences affects but lacks an unconscious: perhaps such an anthropological mutation awaits us in the not-too-distant future. But what affects will it entail?

There is another important issue associated with the matter of desire, one concerning sexuality, erotics,[2] and—more broadly— the role of a person's physical presence or closeness in relations of friendship. With regard to the first, narrower problem, we are encumbered with the legacy of modern bourgeois morality, which compels us to believe that love is the sole justification for erotic contacts, or at least the source of their meaning, without which they remain soulless, mechanical intercourse between bodies. If an erotic element appears in a friendship, it ceases to be a friendship, and may turn into love (integrated with sexuality), which it was destined to become anyway, if—in the case of heterosexuals—it is a famously impossible friendship between a man and a woman.[3] The concept of "friends with benefits" has become common parlance, but we are still unready to combine the two in theory and practice, unless we take it to mean "sex with no (emotional) strings attached." This is because friendship is about just that: emotional involvement, but in a way that differs from love in a few crucial points. One is that the non-possessive nature of friendship means that it lacks the element of monopoly or exclusivity. This, in turn, points us to the issue of sexual exclusivity, monogamy and (perhaps not quite so) new practices such as polyamory. Despite its name, the latter is not about the multiplication of love (in the romantic sense), but about relations of another type, ones more similar to those shared by "friends with benefits," maintained with many people, with their knowledge and approval. There was already something similar in the slogan of free love, which wasn't just about embracing promiscuity, but also, and perhaps more importantly, love and erotics free from neurosis. But there are also many differences between the countercultural praise of free love and polyamory. The most important among them is that while the former was associated with the desire to "change the world" and with more or less overt hostility toward (petite-) bourgeois morality, the latter is essentially happy to carve out a safe niche for itself and be tolerated within the existing society, even if it does not look kindly on such experimentation. This is likely dictated in part by strategic considerations, or rather tactical ones (the times are not favorable for radicalism), but it is also a result of the different social dynamics involved in both phenomena. I wouldn't go as far as to claim that polyamory is itself "petite-bourgeois" (a charge that is dangerously similar to Stalin's argument against sexual freedom), but it doesn't appear to pose a real threat to the model of the monogamous couple. Phenomena of this sort can be regarded as a kind of sign. Their direct effect on mainstream reality is insignificant, but they are a signal that the times, as they say, are changing. And they will continue to change. Friendship, love, sexuality, and how we conceive and raise children: all of these elements (and a couple of others), as is apparent by looking at the history and cultural-geographical dispersal of the human race, and the sheer variety of "family" models that exist in different cultures, etc., form complex configurations and nexuses that inevitably come undone from time to time, only to reform new connections. As Derrida writes, while it will always be necessary for there to exist *"something of* a family, some social bond organized around procreation" or "the familial," the actual forms of this organization are mutable and arbitrary. "There is so much that can be done with a man and a woman!...We can imagine so many 'familial' configurations!"[4] In any case, this is certainly a *longue durée* history.

But what role does the element of physical closeness, not necessarily in the erotic sense, play in friendship? Is friendship—

despite my emphasis on the aspect of distance that sets it apart from possessive, engulfing love—not premised on being with each other in the sense of a corporeal, tangible presence? And is this not one of the reasons why it is so hard for people to be friends in this era of "virtual reality" and long-distance interaction through social media? Here the matter is more complicated. I decided not to address this theme in the essay, so as not to fall into the clichéd trap of hurriedly tacking on a few paragraphs or footnotes about the Internet and digital life as new phenomena that demand our consideration. These phenomena are no longer new and appear to be well-studied in a number of discourses, from neurophysiology, through communications studies, to psychology; it remains a fact, however, that we still know very little about the cultural and anthropological shift we are witnessing today. To avoid repeating the above cliché in this afterword, let me conclude by offering one observation regarding friendship online. There have certainly been instances of long-distance, epistolary friendships throughout history. These can even form between people who have never met in person. Our sense that Facebook friends are more *acquaintances* than *friends* is therefore not so much a result of the virtual nature of this communication channel, but likely a consequence of other factors, ones reinforced—but not necessarily directly determined—by technology. I am referring in particular to narcissism. This is one of the issues that I probably dismiss too readily in the essay, hoping to keep its framework intact and stay focused on its main themes—in this case, that of neurosis. It is possible that the personality of our times is becoming just as narcissistic as it was previously neurotic. This would not bode well for the culture of friendship...

Endnotes

Chapter 1 How to Live Together

1 Barthes, *How to Live Together*, xi.

2 Ibid., xii.

3 Cf. ibid., xxvii.

4 Although the word "family" began to be used in France to refer to a father, mother, and children in the late seventeenth century, this would not become the basic meaning of the term until much later. As Jean-Louis Flandrin writes, "What was referred to in past times as the 'family' was not identical to the father–mother-children triad," and therefore "one cannot study this triad, in the sixteenth, seventeenth and eighteenth centuries, without taking into account its relation with *lignage* or kindred on the one hand, and the domestic staff on the other" (Flandrin, *Families in Former Times*, 10). The emergence and legitimization of this narrow understanding of the family took place at different rates in different strata of society. See Perrot, *A History of Private Life, Volume IV*, especially Chapter 2, "The Actors," devoted to the family.

5 Michel Foucault uses this term to describe the new, neoliberal form of economic man (*homo economicus*), which is replacing the "trading man" (see Foucault, *The Birth of Biopolitics*).

6 The fluid transition and close ties between these two forms of chauvinism (national and cultural or "civilizational") is best illustrated by the recent creation, in Europe, of a kind of nationalist international. One would be mistaken to seek any contradiction here. The goal of these efforts isn't just to create a "Europe of nations," where each nation entrenches itself to defend its own sovereignty and pride, but to form a common front to guard the "civilization of the white

man." The self-proclaimed saviors of the West speak in an idiom developed largely by radical nationalist movements, and their organizations (such as Pegida, in Germany) are manned by supporters of these movements.

7   See Deleuze and Guattari, *Anti-Oedipus*, 234–236, 251–253.

8   See Hegel, *Elements of the Philosophy of Right*, Part III, Section 2: Civil Society.

9   See Boltanski and Chiapello, *The New Spirit of Capitalism*, 167–215.

10   See Hardt and Negri, *Commonwealth*.

11   *The Advocate* 400 (August 7, 1984). Quoted from "Sex, Power, and the Politics of Identity," in *Michel Foucault, Ethics: Subjectivity and Truth*, 170–171.

12   "Friendship as a Way of Life," 136.

13   Ibid., 136.

14   Ibid.

15   Giddens, *The Transformation of Intimacy*, 14–15, 154.

16   Foucault, "Sex, Power, and the Politics of Identity," 161.

17   Ibid., 170.

18   "If the inmates are convicts, there is no danger of a plot, an attempt at collective escape, the planning of new crimes for the future, bad reciprocal influences; if they are patients, there is no danger of contagion; if they are madmen there is no risk of their committing violence upon one another; if they are schoolchildren, there is no copying, no noise, no chatter, no waste of time; if they are workers, there are no disorders, no theft, no coalitions, none of those distractions that slow down the rate of work, make it less perfect or cause accidents. The crowd, a compact mass, a locus of multiple exchanges, individualities merging together, a collective effect, is abolished and replaced by a collection of separated individualities. From the point of view of the guardian, it is replaced by a multiplicity that can be numbered and supervised; from the point of view of the inmates, by a

sequestered and observed solitude." Foucault, *Discipline and Punish*, 200–201.

19 Vincent-Buffault, *L'exercice de l'amitié*.

20 Ibid., 76, 131.

21 Ibid., 124.

22 See Faderman, *Surpassing the Love of Men* (a book that Foucault happened to be familiar with).

23 Foucault, *The Hermeneutics of the Subject*, Lecture of January 20, 1982.

24 Vincent-Buffault, *L'exercise de l'amitié*, 160.

25 Hahn, "Zur Soziologie der Freundschaft," 68.

26 White, *Christian Friendship in the Fourth Century*, 46–53.

27 Caroline White's study specifically addresses the fourth century CE, but it also contains more general reflections on the complex relations between the Greek and Christian understandings of friendship (see the chapter titled "Some Problems of Christian Fellowship"). The period White studies is particularly interesting in this regard, as it witnesses intense attempts to assimilate, or translate, the legacy of antiquity for the purposes of Christian thought.

28 James and Kent, "Renaissance Friendship."

29 Cf. Fraisse, *Philia. La notion d'amitié dans la philosophie antique* and Konstant, *Friendship in the Classical World*.

Chapter 2 Just Friends?

1 Aristotle, *Nicomachean Ethics*, 1157b.

2 See Xenophon, *The Symposium*, Chapter 8, 18–28.

3 See Plato, *Phaedrus*, 231d: "For they themselves confess that they are insane, rather than in their right mind, and that they know they are foolish, but cannot control themselves."

4 Aristotle, *Nicomachean Ethics*, 1156b.

5 Which Plato expresses emphatically in *The Phaedrus*, in Socrates' second speech, essentially a praise of madness, provided that is ultimately directed not at the body, but at

Beauty Itself.

6   Michel Foucault, *The Use of Pleasure*, 40.

7   Ibid,. Part IV, "Erotics," 185–226.

8   It would be more precise, from the psychoanalytical standpoint, to describe desire as marked by lack, not in the sense of simply being unsatisfied, but due to its structural connection to the phantasm of the impossible jouissance and the Thing that is its source.

9   See Deleuze and Guattari, *Anti-Oedipus*, 67–68: "We are not saying that Oedipus and castration do not amount to anything. We are oedipalized, we are castrated; psychoanalysis didn't invent these operations, to which it merely lends the new resources and methods of its genius… And above all, what brings about our sickness? Schizophrenia itself, as a process? Or is it brought about by the frantic neuroticization to which we have been delivered, and for which psychoanalysis has invented new means—Oedipus and castration?" What is more, according to Deleuze and Guattari, this neuroticization is precisely what introduces lack into desire. In this sense, the connection between desire and love and neurosis, posited here, is substantiated, albeit with the reservation that it is the kind of desire that pursues the phantasm of wholeness. This is not the only form of desire identified by the authors of *Anti-Oedipus*, of course.

10   Freud rejected Jung's notion of the Electra complex as the female counterpart or symmetrical reflection of the Oedipus complex (see Laplanche and Pontalis, *The Language of Psycho-Analysis*, 152).

11   The extent to which this stereotype reflects reality is difficult to determine. Using poetic license rather than actual sociological observations, Michel Houellebecq has a character in his latest novel make the following statement: "They may talk about politics, literature, stocks or sports, depending on the man, but about their love lives they keep

silent, even to their dying breath." Houellebecq, *Submission*, 16.

12 The word *hetairoi* itself does not refer exclusively to combat and a military context. Already in Homeric times, the term was used to describe "companions" participating together in endeavors of various kinds (see Konstant, *Friendship in the Classical World*, chapter titled "Hetairos," 31–33).

13 Klaus Theweleit, *Male Fantasies Volume 2*, chapter titled "The Troop as a Totality-Machine," 153–158. For Theweleit, "aggression is a function of male bonding" (380), at least in groups of soldiers. Perhaps this is not so much friendship as it is something into which male brotherly friendship easily "descends" under certain social-historical circumstances.

14 Fromm, *To Have or to Be?*, 39.

15 Ibid.

16 Horney, *The Neurotic Personality of Our Time*, 115.

17 Ibid., 115–116.

18 Ibid., 118.

19 Ibid., 284.

20 Reich, *The Sexual Revolution. Toward a Self-Regulating Character Structure*, 49.

21 Ibid., 147.

22 See ibid., 149: "The sex reformer states that most marriages are miserable because complete sexual gratification is lacking, because the men are clumsy, the women cold. Therefore he proposes an eroticization of marriage...hoping that this will improve the relations among married people."

23 Ibid., 180.

24 Ibid., 201.

25 See Jenny Diski's vivid—and fundamentally affirmative—descriptions of everyday sexual practices in the 1960s, which reveal, for example, how the patriarchal habits of men did not change in step with the loosening of sexual mores: "My guess, no, my certainty, is that large numbers of people

slept with friends, acquaintances and strangers that they had no desire for. I also guess that this was more desultory for women, few of whom, I regret to say, seemed as jaunty the following day as the men who waved them a cheery farewell." In another passage, Diski offers a bitter reflection of a more general nature: "In order to fight against the arbitrary moral codes the bourgeois world imposed on the young, the young imposed on themselves arbitrary physical requirements that took very little account of the complexity of human emotional connections. We cut a swathe through the conventions, but invented new conventions that gave us just as much heartache" (Diski, *The Sixties*, 60, 62). These words are especially salient given that they are not uttered by a typical remorseful ex-hippy who has disavowed the madness of her youth and joined the cult of firm bourgeois values.

26 Reich, *The Sexual Revolution*, 246.

27 Ibid., 165.

28 Aristotle, *Nicomachean Ethics*, 1155a.

29 Ibid.

30 Aristotle, *Politics*, Book 1, section 1252b.

31 Ibid.

32 Aristotle, *Nicomachean Ethics*, 1155a.

33 Aristotle, *Nicomachean Ethics*, 1157a.

34 Nearly 2000 years after Aristotle, Montaigne summarized in these words the reason behind his great fondness for Étienne de la Boétie, author of the famous *Discourse on Voluntary Servitude*. Montaigne, *The Complete Essays*, 212.

35 Plato, *Lysis*, 207c.

36 Kant, *The Metaphysics of Morals*, 6:469.

37 Ibid., 358.

38 Barthes, *How to Live Together*, 6.

39 The practice of "long-distance" friendship is one of its canonical forms. Already the friendship between Montaigne

and la Boétie—which, in the words of the former, was "so perfect and so entire"—involved very little personal contact (in the later years of the latter's life). The author of the *Essays* describes its beginnings as follows: "We were seeking each other before we set eyes on each other—both because of the reports we each had heard (which made a more violent assault on our emotions than was reasonable from what they had said), and, I believe, because of some decree of Heaven: we embraced each other by repute, and, at our first meeting, which chanced to be at a great crowded town-festival, we discovered ourselves to be so seized by each other, so known to each other and so bound together that from then on none was so close as each was to the other" (Montaigne, *The Complete Essays*, 212).

40 Barthes, *How to Live Together*, 171.

41 Giddens, *The Transformation of Intimacy*.

42 Ibid., 43–44.

43 Cf. ibid., 94.

44 Ibid., 185.

45 Ibid., 43. The idea of this patriarchal division of labor (performed for men by women) of course predates bourgeois society. After all, as Demosthenes said in the fourth century BCE, "We have *hetaerae* for pleasure and concubines for daily needs, wives, however, for providing us legitimate children and for tending to the interior of the household" (quoted in Simmel, *Sociology*, 322).

46 Giddens, *The Transformation of Intimacy*, 137.

Chapter 3 The Pathos of Closeness

1 Diogenes Laertius, *Lives of Eminent Philosophers*, V, 21.

2 Aristotle, *Nicomachean Ethics*, 1158a: "It is not possible to have many friends."

3 Ibid., 1171a.

4 Agamben, "The Friend," 27–28.

5   Derrida, *The Politics of Friendship*. In the above-cited essay about friendship, Agamben reveals that he shared his philological discovery with Derrida, who, to his great surprise, made no mention of it in his book, even though he quotes the original phrasing of Aristotle's statement.

6   Fraisse, *Philia. La notion d'amitié dans la philosophie antique*, 63–64.

7   Aristotle, *Nicomachean Ethics*, 1159b.

8   Ibid., 1161a.

9   Derrida, *The Politics of Friendship*, 237.

10 Konstant, *Friendship in the Classical World*, 28.

11 Derrida, *The Politics of Friendship*, 92.

12 Ibid., 93.

13 This is the paradigmatic understanding, but it is not the only one. Suffice it to mention, after Levinas, the example of Abraham, "who leaves his fatherland forever for a yet unknown land, and forbids his servant to even bring back his son to the point of departure" (Levinas, "The Trace of the Other," 348).

14 Homer, *The Odyssey*, 7:179–181.

15 Plato, *Lysis*, 213d–215c.

16 Ibid., 215c–216b.

17 Ibid., 222b–222e.

18 Ibid., 222e.

19 *Republic*, 590d. In *Laws* (837a–d), Plato makes mention of two types of friendship: the one that "occurs between opposites is terrible and fierce and seldom reciprocal amongst men, while that based on similarity is gentle and reciprocal throughout life." This principle of attraction likely has very ancient roots, and can be found, at any rate, in Homer (see *The Odyssey*, 17:237: "Dirt finds dirt by the will of god!").

20 Aristotle, *Nicomachean Ethics*, 1156b.

21 Ibid., 1169b.

22 Derrida, *The Politics of Friendship*, 104.

23 Derrida, *Specters of Marx*, 212.

24 Schmitt, *The Concept of the Political*, 27.

25 Derrida, *The Politics of Friendship*, 76–77.

26 Abramowski, "O związkach przyjaźni," 358.

27 One example worth mentioning here is Saint-Just's project to institutionalize friendship as revolutionary and republican virtue. Anyone "who says that he does not believe in friendship, or who has no friends," would receive no lesser punishment that banishment (excerpt from Saint-Just's *Republican Institutions*, in *Readings in European History, Volume II*, 453). Furthermore, "every man twenty-one years of age" would be required to "publicly state in the temple who are his friends," and then renew that declaration each year. If he were to desert his friend, he would be "bound to explain his motives before the people in the temples" (ibid.). The character of these rituals is as bizarre as it is ominous, especially once the rule of collective punishment is added to them: "If a man commits a crime, his friends shall be banished" (ibid.). Cf. Vincent-Buffault, *L'exercise de l'amitié*, 110–112.

28 This would probably be the more contemporary meaning of Montaigne's formula ("Because it was him; because it was me") and, more generally, "being oneself": "him" and "me" are not mutually identical substances, but "sites of becoming."

29 Aristotle considers the reasons for which a friendship could be broken off, and associates them primarily with matters of "virtue" ("Again, supposing we have admitted a person to our friendship as a good man, and he becomes, or we think he has become, a bad man: are we still bound to love him?"), *Nicomachean Ethics*, 1165b. Cf. also *Letters of Marcus Tullius Cicero with His Treatises on Friendship and Old Age*, 34–36.

30 It is all the more urgent to perform a thorough critical analysis of the discourse of the "clash of civilizations."

This concerns not just the book by Samuel Huntington, but the increasingly popular mode of thinking, the new civilizational doxa that this book created and expresses in equal measure. One strategy for its deconstruction might resemble that employed by Derrida with regard to Fukuyama and his "end of history" (see Derrida, *Specters of Marx*, 70–86). Although Fukuyama and Huntington's global bestsellers, published a mere 4 years apart (in 1992 and 1996), ostensibly posit contradictory diagnoses—the triumph of "liberal democracy" on the one hand, and on the other the return of history in the form of a potentially bloody conflict between "the West and Islam" (see Huntington, *The Clash of Civilizations and the Remaking of World Order*, 209–218)—they share an oversimplified, if not simplistic, way of thinking, with more or less implicit allusions to philosophical traditions. Both also offer seemingly coherent explanations of all subsequent historical facts, which are supposed to simply support the assumptions made in the books.

31 Houellebecq, *Submission*, 127.

32 Theweleit, *Das Lachen der Täter*, 107–108.

33 The initial hypothesis, according to which the "culture of friendship" has been in decline, or at least in crisis, since the turn of the eighteenth and nineteenth centuries, should perhaps be modified. It is true that politics based on the "pathos of closeness" appeals today to motifs developed by modern nationalism, but its genealogy (as interrupted and discontinuous as it may be) has roots running back to much earlier eras. The same is true of the rationale of human dominion, even if it took on a new, more radical form during the Industrial Revolution. The question is, how exactly do these immediate and more remote genealogies overlap?

34 Klein, *This Changes Everything*.

Afterword

1 Here the concept of the internal and external is relative to the extent that a family/couple bound internally by bonds of friendship would no longer be compelled to compulsively guard and entrench themselves in their boundaries, while work based on cooperation would no longer be something from which we longed to free ourselves in order to live "a more human life," if only for a moment. The latter, however, is even harder to imagine, especially since contemporary capitalism has co-opted the very notion of cooperation, effortlessly reconciling it with competition ("coopetition"), and even with alienation and exploitation.

2 The conceptual distinction between these two categories is very important and stems precisely from the connection between sexuality and desire.

3 The widespread conviction that such relationships are impossible is probably one of the most pessimistic bits of folk (and conventional) psychology. As if two halves of humanity were doomed by nature to perform an endless, clumsy mating dance...

4 Jacques Derrida, Elisabeth Roudinesco, *For What Tomorrow...*, 36–37.

References

Abramowski, Edward. "O związkach przyjaźni." In *Pisma*, vol. 1. Warsaw: Związek Spółdzielni Spożywców Rzeczypospolitej Polskiej, 1924.

Agamben, Giorgio. "The Friend." In *What is an Apparatus,* translated by David Kishik and Stefan Pedatella, 25–38. Stanford: Stanford University Press, 2009.

Aristotle. *Nicomachean Ethics,* translated by H. Rackham. Cambridge: Harvard University Press, 1934.

Aristotle. *Politics,* translated by H. Rackham. Cambridge: Harvard University Press, 1944.

Barthes, Roland. *How to Live Together,* translated by Kate Briggs. New York: Columbia University Press, 2012.

Boltanski, Luc and Ève Chiapello. *The New Spirit of Capitalism,* translated by Gregory Elliott. London: Verso, 2005.

Cicero. *Letters of Marcus Tullius Cicero with His Treatises on Friendship and Old Age; Letters of Pliny the Younger,* translated by Evelyn Shirley Shuckburgh, William Melmoth, Frederick Charles Tindal Bosanquet. New York: Cosimo Classics, 2010.

Deleuze, Gilles and Félix Guattari. *Anti-Oedipus: Capitalism and Schizophrenia,* translated by Robert Hurley, Mike Seem, and Helen R. Lane. Minneapolis: Minnesota University Press, 1983.

Derrida, Jacques and Elisabeth Roudinesco. *For What Tomorrow...A Dialogue.* Stanford: Stanford University Press, 2004.

Derrida, Jacques. *The Politics of Friendship,* translated by George Collins. London: Verso, 2005.

Derrida, Jacques. *Specters of Marx: The State of the Debt, the Work of Mourning and the New International,* translated by Peggy Kamuf. London: Routledge, 1994.

Diogenes Laertius. *Lives of Eminent Philosophers,* translated by

R.D. Hicks. Cambridge: Harvard University Press, 1972.

Diski, Jenny. *The Sixties*. London: Profile Books, 2009.

Faderman, Lillian. *Surpassing the Love of Men. Romantic Friendship and Love between Women from the Renaissance to the Present.* New York: William Morrow & Company, 1981.

Flandrin, Jean-Louis. *Families in Former Times. Kinship, Household and Sexuality*, translated by Richard Southern. Cambridge: Cambridge University Press, 1979.

Foucault, Michel. "Friendship as a Way of Life." In *Michel Foucault, Ethics: Subjectivity and Truth*, vol. 1, edited by Paul Rabinow, translated by Robert Hurley et al., 135–140. New York: The New Press, 1997.

Foucault, Michel. *The Hermeneutics of the Subject. Lectures at the College de France, 1981–82*, translated by Graham Burchell. New York: Palgrave Macmillan, 2005.

Foucault, Michel. *Discipline and Punish: The Birth of the Prison*, translated by Alan Sheridan. New York: Vintage, 2012.

Foucault, Michel. *The Birth of Biopolitics. Lectures at the College de France, 1978–1979*, translated by Michel Senellart. New York: Palgrave Macmillan, 2011.

Foucault, Michel. "Sex, Power, and the Politics of Identity." In *Michel Foucault, Ethics: Subjectivity and Truth*, edited by Paul Rabinow, translated by Robert Hurley et al., 170–171. New York: The New Press, 1997.

Foucault, Michel. *The Use of Pleasure. Volume 2 of The History of Sexuality*, translated by Robert Hurley. New York: Vintage, 1990.

Fraisse, Jean-Claude. *Philia. La notion d'amitié dans la philosophie antique*. Paris: Vrin, 1974.

Fromm, Erich. *To Have or to Be?*. London: Bloomsbury, 2012.

Giddens, Anthony. *The Transformation of Intimacy: Sexuality, Love and Eroticism in Modern Societies*. Stanford: Stanford University Press, 1992.

Hahn, Alois, "Zur Soziologie der Freundschaft." In *Freundschaft*.

Theorien und Poetiken, edited by K. Münchberg and C. Reidenbach, 67–77. Munich: Wilhelm Fink Verlag, 2012.

Hardt, Michael and Antonio Negri. *Commonwealth*. Cambridge: Harvard University Press, 2009.

Hegel, G.W.F. *Elements of the Philosophy of Right*, edited by Allen Wood, translated by Hugh Barr Nisbet. Cambridge: Cambridge University Press, 2003.

Homer. *The Odyssey*, translated by Robert Fagles. New York: Penguin Books, 1997.

Horney, Karen. *The Neurotic Personality of Our Time*. Oxford: Routledge, 1999.

Houellebecq, Michel. *Submission*, translated by Lorin Stein. London: William Heinemann, 2015.

Huntington, Samuel. *The Clash of Civilizations and the Remaking of World Order*. London: Touchstone Books, 1998.

James, Carolyn and Bill Kent. "Renaissance Friendship: Traditional Truths, New and Dissenting Voices." In *Friendship. A History*, edited by Barbara Cane, 111–164. London: Equinox, 2009.

Kant, Immanuel. *The Metaphysics of Morals*, translated and edited by Mary J. Gregor. Cambridge: Cambridge University Press, 1996.

Klein, Naomi. *This Changes Everything: Capitalism vs. The Climate*. New York: Simon & Schuster, 2014.

Konstant, David. *Friendship in the Classical World*. Cambridge: Cambridge University Press, 1997.

Xenophon. *The Symposium*, translated by E.C. Marchant. In *Xenophon in Seven Volumes, 4*. Cambridge: Harvard University Press, 1979.

Laplanche, Jean and J.-B. Pontalis. *The Language of Psycho-Analysis*, translated by Donald Nicholson-Smith. London: Karnac Books, 1988.

Levinas, Emmanuel. "The Trace of the Other," translated by Alphonso Lingis. In *Deconstruction in Context*, edited by Mark

Taylor, 345-359. Chicago: University of Chicago Press, 1986.

Montaigne, Michel. *The Complete Essays*, translated and edited by M.A. Screech. New York: Penguin Classics, 1993.

Perrot, Michelle (ed.). *A History of Private Life, Volume IV: From the Fires of Revolution to the Great War*, translated by Arthur Goldhammer. Cambridge: Belknap Press, 1994.

Plato. *Phaedrus*. In *Plato in Twelve Volumes, Volume 9*, translated by Harold N. Fowler. Cambridge: Harvard University Press, 1925.

Plato. *Lysis*. In *Plato in Twelve Volumes, Volume 8*, translated by W.R.M. Lamb. Cambridge: Harvard University Press, 1955.

Plato. *Republic*. In *Plato in Twelve Volumes, Volume 5 & 6*, translated by Paul Shorey. Cambridge: Harvard University Press, 1969.

Plato. *Laws*. In *Plato in Twelve Volumes, Volume 10 & 11*, translated by R.G. Bury. Cambridge: Harvard University Press, 1967 and 1968.

Reich, Wilhelm. *The Sexual Revolution. Toward a Self-Regulating Character Structure*. New York: Farrar, Straus & Giroux, 1974.

Saint-Just, Louis Antoine, *Republican Institutions*. In *Readings in European History, Volume II*, edited by James Harvey Robinson. Boston: Gin & Company, 1906.

Schmitt, Carl. *The Concept of the Political*, translated by George Schwab. Chicago: University of Chicago Press, 2007.

Simmel, Georg. *Sociology*, translated and edited by Anthony J. Blasi, Anton K. Jacobs, Mathew Kanjirathinkal. Leiden, Boston: Brill, 2009.

Theweleit, Klaus, *Male Fantasies, Volume 2*, translated by Erica Carter and Chris Turner. Minneapolis: University of Minnesota Press, 2003.

Theweleit, Klaus. *Das Lachen der Täter: Breivik u.a. Psychogramm der Tötungslust*. St. Pölten – Salzburg – Wien : Residenz Verlag, 2015.

Vincent-Buffault, Anne. *L'exercise de l'amitié. Pour une histoire des pratiques amicales aux XVIIIe et XIXe siècles*. Paris: Seuil, 1995.

White, Carolinne. *Christian Friendship in the Fourth Century.* Cambridge: Cambridge University Press, 1992.

CULTURE, SOCIETY & POLITICS

The modern world is at an impasse. Disasters scroll across our smartphone screens and we're invited to like, follow or upvote, but critical thinking is harder and harder to find. Rather than connecting us in common struggle and debate, the internet has sped up and deepened a long-standing process of alienation and atomization. Zer0 Books wants to work against this trend. With critical theory as our jumping off point, we aim to publish books that make our readers uncomfortable. We want to move beyond received opinions.

Zer0 Books is on the left and wants to reinvent the left. We are sick of the injustice, the suffering and the stupidity that defines both our political and cultural world, and we aim to find a new foundation for a new struggle.

If this book has helped you to clarify an idea, solve a problem or extend your knowledge, you may want to check out our online content as well. Look for Zer0 Books: Advancing Conversations in the iTunes directory and for our Zer0 Books YouTube channel.

Popular videos include:

Žižek and the Double Blackmain

The Intellectual Dark Web is a Bad Sign

Can there be an Anti-SJW Left?

Answering Jordan Peterson on Marxism

Follow us on Facebook
at https://www.facebook.com/ZeroBooks and Twitter at https://
twitter.com/Zer0Books

Bestsellers from Zer0 Books include:

Give Them An Argument
Logic for the Left
Ben Burgis
Many serious leftists have learned to distrust talk of logic. This is
a serious mistake.
Paperback: 978-1-78904-210-8 ebook: 978-1-78904-211-5

Poor but Sexy
Culture Clashes in Europe East and West
Agata Pyzik
How the East stayed East and the West stayed West.
Paperback: 978-1-78099-394-2 ebook: 978-1-78099-395-9

An Anthropology of Nothing in Particular
Martin Demant Frederiksen
A journey into the social lives of meaninglessness.
Paperback: 978-1-78535-699-5 ebook: 978-1-78535-700-8

In the Dust of This Planet
Horror of Philosophy vol. 1
Eugene Thacker
In the first of a series of three books on the Horror of Philosophy,
In the Dust of This Planet offers the genre of horror as a way of
thinking about the unthinkable.
Paperback: 978-1-84694-676-9 ebook: 978-1-78099-010-1

The End of Oulipo?
An Attempt to Exhaust a Movement
Lauren Elkin, Veronica Esposito
Paperback: 978-1-78099-655-4 ebook: 978-1-78099-656-1

Capitalist Realism
Is There No Alternative?
Mark Fisher
An analysis of the ways in which capitalism has presented itself
as the only realistic political-economic system.
Paperback: 978-1-84694-317-1 ebook: 978-1-78099-734-6

Rebel Rebel
Chris O'Leary
David Bowie: every single song. Everything you want to know,
everything you didn't know.
Paperback: 978-1-78099-244-0 ebook: 978-1-78099-713-1

Kill All Normies
Angela Nagle
Online culture wars from 4chan and Tumblr to Trump.
Paperback: 978-1- 78535-543-1 ebook: 978-1-78535-544-8

Cartographies of the Absolute
Alberto Toscano, Jeff Kinkle
An aesthetics of the economy for the twenty-first century.
Paperback: 978-1-78099-275-4 ebook: 978-1-78279-973-3

Malign Velocities
Accelerationism and Capitalism
Benjamin Noys
Long listed for the Bread and Roses Prize 2015, *Malign Velocities*
argues against the need for speed, tracking acceleration
as the symptom of the ongoing crises of capitalism.
Paperback: 978-1-78279-300-7 ebook: 978-1-78279-299-4

Meat Market
Female Flesh under Capitalism
Laurie Penny
A feminist dissection of women's bodies as the fleshy fulcrum of
capitalist cannibalism, whereby women are both consumers and
consumed.
Paperback: 978-1-84694-521-2 ebook: 978-1-84694-782-7

Babbling Corpse
Vaporwave and the Commodification of Ghosts
Grafton Tanner
Paperback: 978-1-78279-759-3 ebook: 978-1-78279-760-9

New Work New Culture
Work we want and a culture that strengthens us
Frithjoff Bergmann
A serious alternative for mankind and the planet.
Paperback: 978-1-78904-064-7 ebook: 978-1-78904-065-4

Romeo and Juliet in Palestine
Teaching Under Occupation
Tom Sperlinger
Life in the West Bank, the nature of pedagogy and the role of a
university under occupation.
Paperback: 978-1-78279-637-4 ebook: 978-1-78279-636-7

Ghosts of My Life
Writings on Depression, Hauntology and Lost Futures
Mark Fisher
Paperback: 978-1-78099-226-6 ebook: 978-1-78279-624-4

Sweetening the Pill
or How We Got Hooked on Hormonal Birth Control
Holly Grigg-Spall
Has contraception liberated or oppressed women?
Sweetening the Pill breaks the silence on the dark side of hormonal
contraception.
Paperback: 978-1-78099-607-3 ebook: 978-1-78099-608-0

Why Are We The Good Guys?
Reclaiming your Mind from the Delusions of Propaganda
David Cromwell
A provocative challenge to the standard ideology that Western
power is a benevolent force in the world.
Paperback: 978-1-78099-365-2 ebook: 978-1-78099-366-9

The Writing on the Wall
On the Decomposition of Capitalism and its Critics
Anselm Jappe, Alastair Hemmens
A new approach to the meaning of social emancipation.
Paperback: 978-1-78535-581-3 ebook: 978-1-78535-582-0

Enjoying It
Candy Crush and Capitalism
Alfie Bown
A study of enjoyment and of the enjoyment of studying. Bown asks what enjoyment says about us and what we say about enjoyment, and why.
Paperback: 978-1-78535-155-6 ebook: 978-1-78535-156-3

Color, Facture, Art and Design
Iona Singh
This materialist definition of fine-art develops guidelines for architecture, design, cultural-studies and ultimately social change.
Paperback: 978-1-78099-629-5 ebook: 978-1-78099-630-1

Neglected or Misunderstood
The Radical Feminism of Shulamith Firestone
Victoria Margree
An interrogation of issues surrounding gender, biology, sexuality, work and technology, and the ways in which our imaginations continue to be in thrall to ideologies of maternity and the nuclear family.
Paperback: 978-1-78535-539-4 ebook: 978-1-78535-540-0

How to Dismantle the NHS in 10 Easy Steps (Second Edition)
Youssef El-Gingihy
The story of how your NHS was sold off and why you will have to buy private health insurance soon. A new expanded second edition with chapters on junior doctors' strikes and government blueprints for US-style healthcare.
Paperback: 978-1-78904-178-1 ebook: 978-1-78904-179-8

Digesting Recipes
The Art of Culinary Notation
Susannah Worth
A recipe is an instruction, the imperative tone of the expert, but
this constraint can offer its own kind of potential. A recipe need
not be a domestic trap but might instead offer escape – something
to fantasise about or aspire to.
Paperback: 978-1-78279-860-6 ebook: 978-1-78279-859-0

Most titles are published in paperback and as an ebook.
Paperbacks are available in traditional bookshops. Both print and
ebook formats are available online.
Follow us on Facebook
at https://www.facebook.com/ZeroBooks
and Twitter at https://twitter.com/Zer0Books